What Are You Thinking?

How to Become More Intentional, Deliberate and Conscious with Your Thoughts

By Darius "The Professor" Wise

What Are You Thinking?
How to Become More Intentional, Deliberate and Conscious with Your Thoughts

ISBN-13: 978-1-7326259-0-7
ISBN-10: 1-7326259-0-5

www.IAmDariusWise.com
WiseDecisions, LLC
9103 Woodmore Centre Dr.
Suite 348
Lanham, Md 20706
Info@Wise-Decisions.com
Copyright © 2018 by Darius A. Wise

All rights reserved. This book is protected by the copyright laws of the United States of America. No part of this book may be reproduced or transmitted in any form for commercial gain or profit without written permission from WiseDecisions, LLC.

Printed in USA.

Dedication

I dedicate this book to my phenomenal wife and love of my life, Allison, who has always been my biggest cheerleader and had a huge part in this book becoming a reality.

Acknowledgments

I would like to thank my parents, Freeman and Sheila, for always supporting me. I appreciate all that you have done for me and loving me like only parents could.

To my kids, Quaashie, Brianna, Amirah and DJ. Thank you for being so kind and sharing me with the world. You all give me life. I pray my actions and these words encourage you to live your best life and always go after your dreams.

Special thank you to Tamera Adams and Dr. Denice O'Sullivan for your amazing wordsmithing. You both have helped me add power and positive energy to my words.

To my family and friends, you all have encouraged me to keep pushing forward. I don't think you know how you have blessed me. Thank you to you all!

To all of my mentors over the years, you all have inspired me to do what is necessary to be the best version of myself. My sincerest thank you to you all!

Thank you, God, for blessing me with the ability to share my gift!

Table of Contents

Foreword 7
Introduction 9
Chapter 1 Who is Responsible for Your Life? 15
Chapter 2 You are What You Think 25
Chapter 3 You Have Been Misdiagnosed 33
Chapter 4 What Do You Know? 39
Chapter 5 Be Careful What You Fight For 45
Chapter 6 I Quit 51
Chapter 7 The "How" Doesn't Matter if… 59
Chapter 8 The Equation That Changes Everything 67
Chapter 9 The Great "*I AM*" 73
Chapter 10 Be Curious 81
Chapter 11 What Did You Expect? 89
Chapter 12 I Hear Voices 97
Chapter 13 That's Not Mine 105
Chapter 14 They're Giving Away Average 111
Chapter 15 Garbage In, Garbage Stays 117
Chapter 16 Did You Want That? 125
Chapter 17 Start First, Learn During 133
Chapter 18 Everything You Do Matters 141
Chapter 19 Constant Contradiction 149
Chapter 20 Why Me? 157
Chapter 21 Coincidence or Confirmation 165
About the Author 173

Foreword

"We cannot solve our problems with the same thinking we used when we created them." ~Albert Einstein

It takes foresight and insight to become our best selves when there are constant forces, both seen and unseen, programming us to be average. We are kept in a constant cycle of habits and thinking that takes no energy to implement yet keep us feeling unaccomplished, frustrated and ultimately unfulfilled.

The truth is, thinking successfully and thus being successful in our personal and professional lives takes WORK. Thinking is a skill to be developed and with intention. It requires an investment of time and mental energy to become a disciplined and strategic thinker—moving the needle forward in every area of our lives.

Einstein said it best, "Thinking is hard work; that's why so few do it."

But not you! By reading the words on this page, you know that your mind is a tool to be sharpened and developed. You are by nature a student of success! By embarking upon this journey with the author of this book,

What are you Thinking?

Darius Wise, you will develop mental pathways of success and growth, to evolve into the highest version of yourself.

As a neuroscientist, mindset success catalyst, entrepreneur, mother, and wife, I know the power of training our brains and minds to reach our highest levels of success, compassion and humanity. Be open as the author takes you on a mental odyssey of successful thinking and practice. Enjoy the journey!

Thank you, Darius Wise, for having the wisdom, courage and foresight to change the world by empowering minds.

Foreword by Shonté Jovan Taylor
Neuroscientist, Entrepreneur
& Mindset Success Trainer

Introduction

So, let me ask you:

Do you think about what you think about?

If I asked this question to my 20, or even 30, year old self, I would have answered with an affirmative "NO." Today, however, my answer is a definite "yes." Why is this important? Because, I have learned that becoming more intentional and deliberate with my conscious thoughts has helped me grow in every area of my life.

Twenty years ago I had a thought. That thought was, "I should write a book!" At that time, I had only been out of college for a few years and I didn't know anyone who had ever written a book. The title I came up with for my book was "What are You Thinking?"

Yes, I had this book idea bouncing around in my head for many years. I was excited when I first had this epiphany. I thought to myself, "how cool would it be to write a book?"

Back then, I had become infatuated with some amazing motivational and inspirational speakers. Individuals like Les Brown, Zig Zigglar, Jim Rohn, and Jack Canfield to name a few.

I listened to their speeches, over and over again until I knew every word. Amazingly my thoughts began to change. I started to see things around me differently. I began to feel differently about the world around me.
This made me curious. What else could I learn? How could I use and apply this information to create the life of my dreams? Were there other speakers that could teach me new ways to think?

Then I had the opportunity to go to a seminar and see a gentleman by the name of George Zalucki. Mr. Zalucki studied motivational psychology and human emotions. He was, and still is, a top Network Marketer and personal development trainer. His voice commanded your attention and as he spoke to the crowd, I sat on the edge of my seat hanging on to his every word. That day Mr. Zalucki broke down how our minds work. He simply said, "Your mind has two parts, the Thinker and the Prover." That was the moment when I knew my mission was to help people understand how they think.

Over the next 20 years, I made many attempts to write my best seller. Somehow, I was never able to write more than a few uninspiring paragraphs. I was frustrated, and I couldn't understand why I was having so much trouble writing. After years of struggling with this challenge, I mentally buried the idea of being an author. In my mind, writing a book was a daunting and overwhelming task.

Introduction

Looking back, I am clear that I allowed life to beat the dream out of me. It wasn't until recently, that I discovered that I wasn't the person I needed to be, back then, to write this book. There was a lot of mental growing I needed to do.

After several years of working on me, the dream had been uncovered. There were bumps in the road along the way, but I learned to focus my mind on my dream. With the help of many books, seminars and mentors I learned how to avoid being distracted by distractions.

In January of 2017, I was introduced to online radio. A good friend of mine named Ginger "Snaps" Cornwell, called me and asked if I would be interested in hosting an online radio show. This was not on my radar prior to her call. She was familiar with trainings I had done in the past and videos I had been sharing on social media.

After a brief moment of thought, I excitedly agreed to host the show. That day "WiseWordsWithDarius" was created. Every Saturday, from 10:00am – 11:00am I was on the air live, sharing what I had learned on my journey of working on me.

After a few episodes, the idea of writing a book returned. It came back with a vengeance. I couldn't stop thinking about this book. The ironic thing about it was that I had the same title idea for the book.

Now, I have hundreds of people listening to me every week. There were some amazing conversations had on those radio shows. But, I still couldn't write more than a couple paragraphs for the book.

I had an idea of how I wanted the book to read and flow. The issue I was having is that the way I envisioned the book was not how most books were written. This perplexed me and stopped me in my tracks. I didn't want to write something that I wouldn't want to read.

Then one Saturday morning, after I finished my radio show my wife, Allison, and I were talking. I shared with her that I wanted to write this book but wasn't having much success getting it going. She looked at me and then at a stack of papers on the desk and said, "there's your book."

That stack of papers were the notes I prepared each week before every show. She realized that the idea I had for the book was how I hosted my radio show every week.

Bing...the light bulb turned on. I said, "you're right, that is the book." I had unconsciously programmed my mind over the years to believe I couldn't write a book. What a lie! To my surprise, the book sat right before my very eyes. I had already done it. That stack of papers became the book you hold in your hands now.

Over the years, I have read hundreds of books. Many of those books I struggled to get through because I just felt they were too theoretical. There were too many irrelevant stories, the chapters were too long and most never gave me what I considered realistic, actionable steps.

With that in mind, I present to you *"What are You Thinking? How to Become More Intentional, Deliberate and Conscious with Your Thoughts."* I wrote this book based on what I always wanted in a book. My goal was to infuse success principles with neuroscience in an easy to understand conversation. I share with you how your thoughts, conscious and unconscious, impact what you achieve in life.

The 21 chapters in this book are short and designed to be read in any order. If you have a situation that you are currently going through, and chapter 17 addresses that situation, you don't have to read the first 16 chapters to get to a solution.

Each chapter ends with a section I call "What Now." These are actionable steps you can immediately began to implement into your life. They are based on the principle/concept that was discussed in that chapter. I have included this section because I believe that it is not the hearing or reading of the information that is important, but the implementation of the information that makes a difference.

My mission with this book is to help you become your best self. Becoming your best self requires some major introspection. You may be familiar with this process by the term "soul searching." To grow you will need to dig down deep, beyond the outer layer. If you do, you will find things you didn't know were there. There may be ideas, thoughts, talents, gifts and beliefs you didn't know, or forgot, you had. If you participate fully, I believe you will have breakthroughs in your life after reading this book.

So, wherever you are right now in your life, be it you are just starting your journey, been around the block a few times or are seasoned to perfection, this book will help you begin to "think about what you think about."

My wish for you is to make the rest of your life, the best of your life. Let's get started!

1

Who is Responsible for Your Life?

No one is having a meeting right now to discuss how to make your life better.

Take a minute and seriously ask yourself "Who is responsible for my Life?" If you think about what this question is asking, your answer should be a no-brainer. Outside of the pro-creation actions of your parents bringing you into this world, who is responsible for the life you live? Is there someone who has been placed in charge of what happens in your life?

The answer to the question, "Who is responsible for your life", is YOU. You are totally responsible for your life and what you make of it. This is a foundational principle, and if you plan to have any happiness and success in life you must embrace it. If you want your life to play out a certain way, you want to achieve a specific goal, or if you want to accomplish something in particular…it is completely YOUR responsibility. Regardless of what you may have been told or believe, it's your responsibility to make LIFE happen for you.

As children we are programmed. Our paradigms are programmed by what we are told, what we learn and what we observe. This can be a double-edged sword. On one hand we are told that we can be anything that we want to be in life, but on the other hand, few people tell us it is our responsibility to make it happen. They fail to mention that we have only ourselves to blame if it doesn't work out the way that we would like. We see those around us who are not living their true authentic life blame others for their outcomes. We often do that ourselves. That is because many of us have not been taught to be more self-aware; to understand that the thoughts that we think and the decisions they make determine the trajectory of their lives.

Taking complete responsibility doesn't mean that you have control over everything that happens in your life. It means you take ownership of what happens in your life. For many people, when things don't go their way, it is someone else's fault. They tend to point their finger out toward someone else instead of inward toward themselves. They have become experts at explaining away every problem with reasons and excuses why they can't affect the situation or outcomes in their life.

When you point the finger or blame someone else for what has transpired in your life, you are saying that someone else is responsible. You attempt to remove yourself from holding any responsibility for what manifests. And without taking responsibility, you are all the more likely to look at your life as a failure because you have allowed others to be responsible for your outcomes.

You are responsible for where you are in life. It's not anyone else's fault. If you have had tremendous success in life...it's your fault. If you feel your life has been a huge failure...it's your fault. Our brains are wired to react, and our normal reaction tends to be to place blame. The challenge, knowing this, is to re-wire our brain. Instead of reacting we need to *respond*. Taking complete responsibility for your life requires a conscious response vs. an unconscious reaction.

How and what we think plays an integral part in what we believe and the actions we take. If you don't believe you are worthy of greatness or accomplishment you will take actions to prove that which you believe. From the outside this looks like blame and excuses. This is usually an unconscious process. In this unconscious state we react to life without thinking. This is what Oprah Winfrey calls the "walking dead." To reverse this, we have to pause and consciously think about the outcome we want in life and find ways to respond instead of react.

Not long ago, my oldest son was finishing up college and looking to graduate. A couple weeks before graduation he called me upset. He was not happy about one of his professors, who he felt was trying to prevent him from graduating. There was a misunderstanding of when an assignment was due and a meeting they were supposed to have and it didn't happen when the professor thought it should. My son reached out to the professor and didn't get a timely response. After letting him explain "his side" of the story I asked him a question. My question was "What is your goal?" He paused...and responded, "to graduate." I said great. My next question was "Who's responsibility is it for you to graduate?" Again, he paused...and said "mine." EXACTYLY...it was his responsibility.

His professor gave them what they needed to pass her class and it was his responsibility to do what was necessary. Doing what is necessary sometimes means sacrifice and doing what you may not want to do. My ultimate response to him was that he needed to set up a meeting with this professor and take complete responsibility for his life and graduating. That looked like this: be focused on your goal of graduating and apologize for misunderstanding when things needed to be done. Do not blame her for anything. Be kind and in great spirits and let her know you are willing to do what it takes to make sure you walk across that stage.

Well, guess what, he graduated! I believe that it was because he took complete responsibility for his actions and his goal. He didn't blame his professor and he did what was necessary to accomplish his goal.

If you are not taking full responsibility for your life, you start from the position that the world is doing something to you, instead, you are at cause in your world. This mindset leads you to develop a victim mentality. This victim mentality feeds off of complaining, excuses and not accepting responsibility for the role you have played in what has happened in your life. When you complain you acknowledge that there is a better situation than the one you are in. Understanding that there is a better situation exposes that you haven't harnessed the remarkable power of your mind.

Too often people look outside of themselves for the answers to why their life has become what it is. Many scholars have referenced the power of your thoughts. "You are what you think", "we become what we think about most", and "man is what his thoughts make of him", are just a few quotes that may be familiar to you. The purpose of these sayings is to show that you have full control over your mind. The thoughts you have and actions you take are of your own doing.

You may have said that YOU are responsible for your life. If you did, that is awesome. The next question then becomes: do you actually live your life that way? Do you go about everything in your life taking 100% responsibility? It is easy to say you are responsible, but when things get tough and don't go your way how do you respond?

When things go your way, I'm sure you get excited like a kid running through the water from a hydrant on a hot summer day. Most are quick to stand up and take responsibility for the good things. The issue is how do you feel and what do you do when the opposite happens. Are you still taking full responsibility when things don't go as desired?

Here is a thought to ponder; It takes the same, if not more, energy to think negative thoughts and speak negatively to yourself than it does to think positive thoughts. Based on your upbringing and programming you may not have been encouraged to think about the things you say to yourself. This inner dialog is not just meaningless chatter. Every time you allow the voice in your head to speak without interruption you are programming your mind. If this voice is constantly speaking negatively, telling you it is not your fault, you are not responsible for this or that, you are not to blame, eventually, you will begin to believe these things. Once this is what you believe you will start to take actions based on those beliefs.

Taking 100% responsibility for your life is an inside job. There will always be something going on in the world around you. The decision if it has power over you is yours to make. If you take control of your thinking and embrace the concept of taking responsibility for your life, what happens around you will have less power over you.

You are the only one that can live your life. You are in charge. The most important aspect of taking responsibility for your life is to acknowledge that your life is your responsibility. Blaming someone else, making excuses or complaining does not change the fact that each event that happens in your life is the result of choices you made and are making.

In conjunction with acknowledging that your life is your responsibility, there are and will be certain actions you will need to take. In order to accomplish any goal, you will need particular skills and knowledge. You will also need to maneuver through obstacles that show up during your journey. So, don't think all you have to do is think good, positive thoughts and everything you want will fall in your lap.

Want a promotion on your job? Then, act like, look like and perform like someone who is already in that position. The only thing holding you back, is you. And if things don't happen when you want them to happen, that doesn't mean that they are not going to happen.

Before my speaking career, my radio show "WiseWordsWithDarius" and this book, I was a software trainer. I started a new job years ago and after working there over a year I had implemented several training programs. When I started, they didn't conduct any in-house training. They were sending employees to other training companies to be trained when they had a full-time trainer on staff. So, I didn't think that made sense and that is what I had been doing for years. A short time later, I started the company's first in-house training program as well as other training programs. My training classes were getting rave reviews. The employees were loving the things they were learning, not having to change their daily commute to go to class and they were happy that I was there after class to help when they had questions with their work. If you have ever taken a training class at a training facility you know how challenging it may be to leave class, go back to work and then have questions and not be able to contact your instructor.

After getting amazing feedback and having a positive impact on the company's productivity and employee morale, I felt I deserved a promotion and raise. Unfortunately, my boss didn't share my feelings.

So, here I am facing this question: Who is responsible for your life? I knew I had a choice. I refused to play the victim card and complain about not getting what I felt I deserved.

I decided that I was not going to let someone else dictate what I should have. I wrote a letter to my boss and her boss. This letter stated, in great detail, all that I had done in my first year and a half on the job. I provided training and participant statistics which detailed how much money I had saved the company. I was persistent and refused to complain or blame anyone else. After another year, the company created a new position for me and gave me a huge raise.

This is an example of a situation that most people will feel powerless and allow life to happen to them. They end up stuck in a position that they don't like and feel that they don't have any options.

You always have an option. It's just a question of do you want to go through with what options you have.

Some options may come with being uncomfortable. This may mean, doing something you don't want to do. You may not want to get out of your comfort zone. You have become used to what you have and what you are getting. Even if you don't like it and feel that you deserve more. To avoid these feelings, you just let it go and "go with the flow."

You get to this point where **the pain of change is greater than the pain of staying the same.** I, nor anyone else, profess that change is easy. Taking complete control of your life will come with its challenges. It will not be a walk in the park.

Denzel Washington, said in his acceptance speech at the 2017 Image Awards, "Ease is a greater threat to progress than hardship. So, keep moving, keep learning and keep growing."

When you go through situations that make you uncomfortable you are still growing. You usually grow more, sometimes in character, strength to endure, faith, optimism and success towards fulfilling your dreams. And these are the times when you have to recognize that it is time to get up and take control of your life.

A mentor of mine shared a story with me years ago, that is engrained in my mind forever.

*There was a man whose neighbor was an older man that would be sitting on his porch every day when the man came home from work. The man noticed that his neighbor had a dog that would be howling everyday while they sat on the porch. One day the man asked the old man "what's wrong with your dog?" The old man replied "nothing...he is fine." This was his answer every time the man asked the question. One day the man just couldn't take it anymore...he walked up on the old man's porch and said I am a veterinarian and I know there is something wrong with your dog. The old man, upset about his neighbors constant prying, said "if you must know, he is sitting on a nail." The man looking baffled, asked the old man why doesn't he get up. The old man responded, "**It doesn't hurt enough.**"*

Are you sitting on a nail...and it doesn't hurt enough? When you don't take 100% responsibility for your life it is just like that dog sitting on that nail. You have the choice to continue sitting there or you can get up.

What's your nail? The nail represents your situation. What is that situation that is holding you back from going for what you want. Is it a new job, promotion, a relationship, a business you want to start, a book you want to write? If you are not doing anything to move forward with it, the nail doesn't hurt enough. When I was working that job, and felt I deserved a raise the nail hurt enough. I couldn't just sit there.

We all have many nails in our life. The question we must ask ourselves is "does it hurt enough" to get up. If you don't believe that you are responsible for something that has happened in your life...**Act As If you are**. Act as if you are responsible and respond in a fashion that will guide you toward that thing you want to accomplish. If you are still able to read these words...there's still time.

I'm here to tell you that you can change your direction at any time. First thing that needs to be done, is you need to make a decision. Step up and take responsibility.

If you are ready to take complete control of your life, here is the strategy. This is simple, but not easy. And I encourage you to apply it in your life. Starting today...Take 100% Responsibility for your life. You are the only person who has that ability.

What Now

1. **Identify** (Recognize your nail) – what situation or how is the way you are viewing your situation stopping you.
2. **Own it** – Stop placing blame. How did you play a part in this situation? (This is a challenging step.)
3. **Take action** – what are your options, what small steps can you begin to take.

2

You are What You Think

The greatest journey is the journey of the mind. And this determines the journey of life.

Who and what you have become is exactly what you thought you would become. The incredible power of our thoughts molds us into the person we are. I understand that this may be hard to swallow, but there is no one else to blame. The issue really is that we have been conditioned to not pay enough attention to what we think every second of every day.

Let me ask you a few questions. How much time and energy do you apply to your thinking? Seriously, have you taken time to sit down and think about what you thought about yesterday, or this morning? Have you taken any time to dissect any of those "random thoughts" you've had and figured out why you had them?

We only have thoughts of things that deep down inside we believe are relevant to us. If you are having thoughts of being average and barely getting by or just making it, the reason you are having those thoughts, I believe, is because that is what you believe is relevant to you.

How does this self-talk sound? This is how it may sound: "My apartment is not that bad; I usually get the same parking space out front in the parking lot; If I owned a house it would be so much work and more to clean, higher bills. Or, I like my job, I know exactly what I need to do every day. If I got a new job I would have to learn new skills, I may have a longer commute. I might not like my new boss." So, we talk ourselves out of that new house, or that new job by virtue of the thoughts that we have unconsciously.

Thoughts that people have hold them back more often than thrust them forward. Once you begin to have these types of thoughts they become justifications. You begin to justify why you are not moving ahead and achieving more.

If you are having thoughts of getting that promotion, starting your own business or accomplishing great things, it's not that you are better than anyone else. It's that you believe those things are relevant to you.

Now, don't get me wrong. It takes more than just having the thought to get things done. But it all begins with the thought of being able to do and have what you desire. And remember your thoughts build into beliefs which dictate your actions.

Here's another question for you: Have you become who you thought you would be?

Just think about that. And if not: Why? And if not "did you really THINK you would be something different?" There is a difference between what we think we are capable of and what we see others do.

I have heard many people say, "I never thought this would be my life." This is a statement that is usually based on what and who we have become compared to what and who others have become. For those who make this statement I always want to ask them "What did you THINK your life would be?"

Let's think about this. This is your life! Based on the thoughts you consistently have, your beliefs and the actions you take, what did you really think your life would be? If you have an awful life, an average life or an amazing life it is grounded in your thoughts!

James Allen – Author of - *As A Man Thinketh* said in his book, "As a man thinketh in his heart, so is he. A man is literally what he thinks. His character being the complete sum of all his thoughts." By your own thoughts you will build the weapons to destroy yourself or you will create the tools to build yourself up.

Here is one way this happens. You don't attract what you say you want, you attract what you believe yourself to be. If you have negative thoughts about yourself or others, you will attract negative experiences, or people. If you are positive you will attract positive.

We often hear people say, "if it wasn't for this or if it wasn't for that I would have done this or that." I want you to realize and understand that **"Circumstances don't make**

the man, they reveal him." You are who you are, not because of what has happened to you, but because of how you responded to your circumstances.

One of my mentors from a far, the late great, Mr. Jim Rohn used to say "There is nothing worse than being stupid. Being broke is bad, but being stupid is what's really bad. And what's really, really bad is being broke and stupid. Nothing much worse than that. Unless you're sick. Being sick, broke and stupid that's about as far as you can fall. Unless you're ugly. That would be the ultimate negative life, being ugly, sick, broke and stupid."

I share this with you because first, I think it is hilarious, the ultimate negative life is being "ugly, sick, broke and stupid." That is funny to me. But the real is that the only way any of these things matter is if YOU think you are any of them. If you don't think you are ugly nothing anyone else says will make you think differently. The only way you will think differently is if you decide to think that way. It's truly that simple.

One of the challenges of how we think of ourselves is that early in life we are given assistance in how we should think. This assistance came from those that said they love us and raised us. If you constantly heard that you were ugly or stupid or never going to be anything as you were growing up, after some time you probably began to think you are all those things. Once you begin to have those thoughts and you attach emotions to those thoughts they will become your beliefs, and your beliefs dictate your actions.

These beliefs will be what you base your actions on. Then you will move through life proving what you believe about yourself. Here is where the 2 parts of the mind come into play. The thinker and the prover. The thinker thinks and the prover proves what the thinker thinks.

This is why it is so painful for me to hear parents talk to their kids in a negative, derogatory way. Telling them they are stupid, fat, ugly or anything like that. These kids after a while will begin to believe these things if that is all they hear. And then the parents wonder why their kids take negative actions when they grow up. It's no secret.

But if you were in an environment that was encouraging and inspiring and you heard beautiful positive things about yourself, your thoughts would have been different. If you heard that you are beautiful, amazing, and can accomplish anything you put your mind to, after some time you will begin to think you are all those things. And once you begin to have those thoughts, and attach emotions to them, they will become your beliefs about yourself. These beliefs will be what you base your actions on. Then you will move through life proving what you believe about yourself.

I went to a training class one day for my job and while sitting in this training room I looked up at the instructor and said to myself "I can do that, I can do what he is doing." Now this was surprising because I had never thought about being an instructor or trainer before. But something came over me and I had this desire now to make this change. After the class, I asked the instructor if his company was hiring and he told me he didn't know but gave me the number of someone I could call. His particular company wasn't hiring so I went on a job search. I was actively looking for training companies that were hiring.

After a few weeks I finally got an interview. I'm ready for a new direction in my career. I went in for the interview. The woman who was the hiring manager asked me several questions, all of which I answered. Then she paused and looked at me and she said "you have no experience in this field and we need someone who can hit the ground running. Why should I hire you?" In my mind for a moment I thought about that, that was a great question. My answer to her was "You are correct, I don't have any experience as a trainer. But I believe that I can do it and I am excited about the opportunity. And if you do hire me and give me a chance I guarantee you that I will be your best and most requested instructor in one year."

She looked shocked and stunned when I told her that. But she took a chance on this young fella and offered me the job. I am proud to say that in one year from that interview I was her best and most requested trainer.

Listening to this story you may ask how did I go from sitting in training class to a year later being a trainer? I had no thought or desire to be a trainer before going to that training class. How did all of that happen? How, I thought I could, that's it. And that fueled the belief that I could. Once the idea appeared to me I thought I would be good at it.

I believe that you will not conceive an idea or thought that you are not capable of achieving. Napoleon Hill, author of *Think and Grow Rich,* put it this way **"What the mind of man can Conceive and Believe, it can Achieve."** Whichever way you can internalize it, understand that YOU are the captain! You are in control and it is up to you what happens in your life and what you become.

One of the beautiful things about the mind is that what you think today does not have to be what you think tomorrow. You can change your mind. You can do a complete 180 and take your life into the opposite direction at any moment.

You don't have to be ugly, sick, broke and stupid. You can be whatever you THINK you can be. And what you THINK is solely up to you.

"If there is anything in life that you want to accomplish, it will first begin with a thought!"

What Now

1. **Think about What You Think About** – What you think about is the foundation of who you are and will become. Take time to sit and think about what you think about.
2. **Be aware of your self-talk** – What you say to yourself is crucial in the programming of your unconscious mind. Program it to believe you can accomplish everything you desire. Tell yourself that you are worthy, you have what it takes, and you can do it.
3. **Change what you think about** – Think differently. You have the ability to change your mind at any time, by changing what you think about. You don't need anyone's permission to change how you think of yourself and your life.

3

You Have Been Misdiagnosed

"Error is not a fault of our knowledge, but a mistake of our judgment giving assent to that which is not true."
John Locke

The news show, 60 minutes, aired a story titled "Chess Country." In this segment they talked about and highlighted grade-school chess teams from Franklin County, Mississippi. Franklin County is a rural county in Mississippi where trains don't stop anymore. Half the county is covered by a national forest, the other half it seems by churches. The population is about 7,000 and there are only two stop lights in the entire county and one elementary school.

The segment went on to state, the perception that most people have of Mississippi is that it is the poorest, the dumbest and the fattest state in the union. The people of Franklin County are not a group that you would think of becoming hugely successful people who are going to change the world. Most of the residents work minimum wage jobs (or a couple jobs) just to make ends meet. They don't dream big if they dream at all.

Then one day a tall stranger came to town from Memphis. His goal was to teach the kids how to play chess. Chess? These kids barely knew what checkers were. These were kids who were viewed as "slow", or "dumb" or "just couldn't learn much" by society's standards. The tall stranger, 6 foot 6 Jeff Bulington, affectionately known as Dr. B, showed up after school to teach chess. The kids couldn't understand why someone like him would come to Franklin County.

He had a clever method of teaching the children chess using stories like Little Red Riding Hood to engage them. To the surprise of many, within two years the kids of Franklin County had won the Chess State Championship and two of them finished in the top 10 in the country.

Watching I couldn't help but think, somebody misdiagnosed those kids of Franklin County. They were looked upon as if they couldn't learn anything new. Before Dr. B came to town, most of them believed that to be their fate. They believed that the most they were going to be able to achieve in life was to work for about $8 an hour. Only after having someone believe in them and give them a chance did a good number of those chess playing kids get excited about the opportunity to go to college. Something only two students of the previous graduating high school class had been able to do.

Dr. B made two statements that made me really want to share this story. He was asked "Why come down to the middle of nowhere to teach chess?" His answer was "there are people here, so it's not nowhere...it's somewhere, somewhere that doesn't get a lot of attention." Then he was asked "What did he think about what people thought about the kids before they learned how to play and now that they were winning and doing well?" He responded by saying: **"It tells me that some people got it wrong, that some kids have been underestimated or written off for reasons that are false."**

One of the biggest challenges I see people facing today is not only have they been misdiagnosed but they believe the diagnosis. They have been told something for so long that they begin to take it as truth. It becomes their belief and once that happens your actions follow what you believe.

There are a few lessons in this story that were profound and I believe you need to be aware of them in your own life.

First, there is somebody that is underestimating you. They don't believe that you can be great. And what I have found is that most people are very concerned about what others think of them. They often want to live up to the expectations that others have of them. Even if those expectations are extremely low. If I don't know you personally I know this about you...you were born a genius, but unfortunately, you may have been raised to be average. You are better than you are acting.

Next, Opportunity usually doesn't come wrapped the way you think. For these students, their opportunity was wrapped as a 6-foot-6 older white man. He didn't look like them, he didn't sound like them, he didn't even eat the same things as they did. One of my early mentors once told me that opportunity is usually dressed in work clothes and most people don't recognize it. Be open, because you don't know how your opportunity will be presented to you.

Take yourself out of the box. You may be given an opportunity to do something that you may have never thought of, but it may take you to your ultimate destination.

I started hosting an internet radio talk show in January 2017. This radio show was not on my radar. If I would have been stuck in the box of what I thought I could do I would have missed an amazing opportunity. Stepping out and trusting what the Universe was bringing my way allowed me to grow, expand, and contribute to the lives of others.

How have you been misdiagnosed? Did someone tell you that you didn't have the right look, or did they say you were not smart enough? Maybe they told you that you were not college material or that you're not cute enough or skinny enough. What was it?

Think back over your life and think about some of the decisions you made. Is there a decision that you made that was not truly what you wanted to do? Was that decision based on what someone else thought you should be doing or would be good at doing? That is a misdiagnosis! Have you been told that the dream you had was not something you could achieve? That is a misdiagnosis!

The issue with the misdiagnosis that you may have received is hear it over and over and over, you start to believe it. Once you believe it, your mind HAS to make it a reality. Next you will start to act out this belief and do things to show yourself that the diagnosis was correct. It is now time that you accept that you were misdiagnosed.

This is what I believe to be one of the biggest challenges facing our youth today. Many of our young people have been misdiagnosed and they believe the negative ideas that they have been told. Remember your mind will prove what you believe. This belief is what they are acting out and it will only change once we begin to help them reprogram their minds.

So, let me tell you and our young people, what Dr. B said about those kids in Mississippi, "Someone got it wrong and you have been underestimated or written off for reasons that are false." It took Dr. B approximately two years to get those young people ready to compete, so understand, if this has been your thinking most of your life, it won't change overnight. If you start today and take small, consistent steps to reprogram your mind you will get there.

You have what it takes to be the best YOU!

You have been misdiagnosed and you need a second opinion. My diagnosis is that you are awesome, you are phenomenal, you can accomplish anything that you focus your mind on and commit too.

―――――――――― *What Now* ――――――――――

1. Develop "thick skin" and eliminate concern about what people think of you, if you are pursuing your passion.
2. Create positive thoughts about yourself.
3. Find someone that believes in you, even if it is someone you don't know personally but they share inspiring words.
4. Be patient. Change doesn't happen overnight.

4

What Do You Know?

What you know right now, has gotten you to where you are.

Too often people want to get to the next level in their life using the information they already know. If you are not intentional about continuing to learn new things you will not experience new levels in life.

If you want to grow beyond your current situation you will need to expand your mindset to accept and implement new information. This desire and ability to continue to learn is what Professor of Psychology and Author, Carol Dweck calls a growth mindset. If you have concluded that you know everything that you need to know and you're not open to learning new skills, she calls this a fixed mindset.

Let me ask you, what comes to mind when you think of learning? People will have different thoughts when it comes to their idea of learning. Some may think of a formal setting like school and others may think of training required by their job.

Once I graduated from college I told everyone that I was done with school. The primary reason I went to college was because I was told and conditioned to believe that it was the only way to get a "job" that would pay me the money I needed to live a "good" life. What I actually meant at the time was that I was finished with my formal education. I had no intentions whatsoever to go back to school. I had learned what I thought I needed to move ahead in life and live comfortably. I was a college graduate. A master's degree was not in the plans and a PhD was definitely out of the question.

One of the reasons I felt this way, was because as an "adult" I didn't believe going back to school was going to get me where I wanted to be in life. I had known people who were going back to school for advanced degrees and watched them do something that I know they didn't truly believe was their calling. For them, this was a painful experience and most of them did it because someone else told them they should. "Oh, you want to make more money, then you need a MBA or you need a PhD." At one point, I was given that same advice. Sound familiar?

Now, don't get me wrong, if you are working toward an advanced degree in something that you feel you are called to do, go for it! Put everything you have into it. But understand why you are truly doing it.

I believe that what you know and implement has gotten you to where you are. I also believe that if you knew what it took to be whatever you wanted to be in life, you would be that. Unconsciously, you may already possess the necessary technical skills, but you may not believe that you can do it. Your belief may be more inhibiting than your knowledge and skill level.

When you think about reaching the next level in your life you must understand you will need to learn some new things. The key to learning as an adult is that it's a choice. You have a choice what you learn. As a child, we were practically forced to learn. We didn't have a choice as to going to school or not. Until you were 18 you were going to school or there were consequences and repercussions.

When I think about learning and what I know, I realize that I have learned some concepts and skills by default. Based on where I was, who I was with and what I listened to, I unconsciously learned something. And because of what I unconsciously learned, I made decisions. This is what I call operating on *autopilot*.

What does autopilot look like? Autopilot is operating unconsciously as opposed to being intentional, and consciously aware of your actions. This may allow you to learn basic skills you need to know on your job or to survive, but this method is like walking around with your fingers and toes crossed, your eyes closed and holding your breath. You are just wishing the right things comes your way.

If you are on autopilot, and learning by default, you may find yourself going in the direction of your goals and dreams, if you're lucky. Usually, there is a bigger chance you will find yourself going in the opposite direction and getting further away from your dream.

I was on autopilot, until I heard something that changed my thinking. A few years after college I decided to start a business. At this time, I was still in the mindset that I was finished with school. Then my mentor, at the time, said to me "formal education will make you a living and self-education will make you a fortune."

This was a moment of awakening. I was excited about the part on making a fortune, but the part on self-education changed everything for me. My perception of learning changed that day. What I heard was "you need to continue to learn and educate yourself." That education may come in different forms, but if you want something more than what you currently have, you need to continue to educate yourself.

Until this concept came into my awareness, the thought of learning was painful for me. It was painful because it always felt forced upon me. Now it seemed to show up as an option. From that moment, I came to understand that learning should be intentional, conscious and deliberate.

Learning is now part of my everyday life. It's intentional. I seek opportunities to learn things that will help me on my journey. Whether it be through new experiences, reading books (like this one), watching webinars or attending courses, they all allow me to gain knowledge I need to achieve my goals.

Science studies show that there are many physiological benefits to learning. When we learn beneficial new things:
- The brain builds new connections between neurons (neuroplasticity occurs);

- We receive a rush of the reward chemical called *dopamine,* which makes learning fun and makes you want to repeat the experience;
- The brain neurons move faster, which helps get more *myelin* onto the nerve axons, so the brain feels like it is working more efficiently;
- We slow the onset and progression of Alzheimer's and dementia, as well as just preventing general slowing of your mental faculties.

Therefore, we should continue to stay in a growth mindset. Not just because it will assist us on our journey to achieving our goals, but it also is good for the brain! As you continue to learn, you will find yourself reaping the benefits.

However, it is not just listening to the information that is important, it is the application of that information that makes a difference. So, as you learn be sure that you begin to apply those new skills and concepts on your journey.

I have found that the more I seek knowledge and information, the more opportunities to learn are presented to me. The universe is constantly looking to bring to you what you say you want. If you are putting out that you want to learn, and you want to grow, the opportunities you seek will come your way. Just be open to how they are presented.

One day, my cousin sent me a video about neuroscience. What's fascinating is just prior to receiving the video I mentioned to my wife that I wanted to learn more about how our brains really work. As I watched the video, I realized this was exactly what I wanted to learn. Just before the video ended, there was an offer for an 8-week course that taught neuroscience to individuals who are trainers, entrepreneurs, coaches and those just interested in learning about the brain.

This was what I call "confirmation." I put out into the Universe what I wanted and was looking for and it sent it to me in the form of a video sent by someone who knew I would find it interesting.

I share that story because I want to encourage you to be open to how things may come your way. If I would have ignored that video I would have missed an opportunity that I was looking for.

To achieve what we desire in life there will be skills we need to learn and knowledge we need to obtain. For us to be prepared for the events that will present this knowledge and skills we need to be *intentional, deliberate and conscious* about learning. Moving forward here are a few actions steps to implement into your journey.

What Now

1. **Seek** learning opportunities. Be open to how they appear in your life.
2. **Apply** what you are learning into your routine.
3. **Understand** you're are building new connections in your brain.

5

Be Careful What You Fight For

If you Fight for your limitations, you get to keep them.

Where your focus goes, your energy flows. I want to bring your attention to a few things we are unconsciously fighting for. Being a trainer, speaker and entrepreneur, I speak with people all the time. I have come to realize that we constantly have personal fights going on in our head. Some of these fights we are aware of, but most of them we are not. When I say fight you might automatically think of physical confrontation. This ideology can cloud what is really happening. We have certain thoughts in our mind that often represent what we don't want. We fight for what we don't want, believing that is how you acquire what you do want. Because you may not be clear on what is taking place, you may over look what you are doing and not understand the results that you are creating in your life.

When you think about something that you want out of life what type of thoughts come to mind? I don't mean when you think of something small, something that keeps you in your comfort zone. I'm talking about that goal that you can't accomplish being the person you are currently. If you have big dreams and you are not playing small you are going to have to stretch yourself to achieve that goal. With that in mind, when you think of that *thing* you want, what type of thoughts come to mind?

Whatever thoughts that you have consistently when you think about achieving that goal is what you are fighting for. Understand the thoughts that you have are based on what you believe.

We are seeing people all over the country and the world marching and protesting. Those that you see with their signs and chanting are marching for something they believe. If you asked any of them what they were doing they would tell you they are fighting for what they believe in. They are fighting for their rights, for their beliefs, fighting for who they are and what they want to be.

You are fighting too. Your fight just might not be played out in the streets of the world it may be played out in your mind. When you fight for something, you are typically defending your beliefs and what you believe in. The conflict comes when you are opposed by someone else or even yourself. When that person challenges what you believe, you fight. You fight to get your point across, you fight to be heard, and you fight to defend your belief.

Some of you may be saying "Darius I don't get it, we should fight for what we believe in." I agree, you should. My goal is to point out how you may be fighting for what you believe and what you believe is NOT something that is moving you toward your goal.

How is that? How does that work? Believing in something that is NOT moving you toward your goal. These are what I will call limited beliefs. They usually show up as thoughts about what you are not or don't want. For most people these are BELIEFS that they fight for and don't realize it. When you focus your thoughts and time on "What you are NOT" your energy will flow towards focusing on *what you are not*.

For many years I was in Network Marketing. I loved this industry and business. I was all in and it was good to me. I met some amazing people, many of which are still my friends to this day. But in that business, it requires you to talk to a lot of people. You are always looking for motivated and excited people, folks who want more out of life and looking for a vehicle to take them there. One day I was talking to this young lady and she had expressed to me that she was looking for something else in life and had a few things she wanted to accomplish. I thought "Awesome what I have may be a great opportunity for her, this may help her achieve those goals she had." We set up a time to meet and sit to talk business. We were talking and I shared a little about what I was doing and how it was helping me achieve some goals I had in life. As we are talking I noticed that she was telling me all the things that she was NOT. She starts, I'm not a sales person, I'm not good with people, I'm not focused, I'm not financially able to start a business, I'm not cut out for that...and the list went on and on. I tried to defuse the tirade she was hitting me with but she was adamant about her feelings and beliefs. She was Fighting for what she was not. In her mind, she was explaining to me who she WAS. After a few minutes, I attempted to share with her all the great qualities I saw in her and she thanked me for the kind words and began again to focus on what she was not. Needless to say, after this meeting we did not partner up in business and I walked away with a new principle. *"**If you FIGHT for your limitations, you get to keep them**"*

When your beliefs are limiting beliefs, you will fight just as hard for them. Most people don't realize that they have these self-limiting beliefs and don't know the power of their words. When I attempted to share the great things I saw in this young lady she fought for her beliefs. They were limiting beliefs, but she fought hard for them. When you are set to go to war for what you believe it is hard for anyone to get you to see something different. The people who are marching for what they believe in are not going to be easily sold a new idea.

When you lack the awareness that you have limiting beliefs you unconsciously fight for what you don't want. Becoming conscious of our thoughts allows us the ability to change our focus. Instead of focusing on what we don't want or what we are not we can redirect our attention to what we are, what we have and what we want.

I was listening to a story of a woman who was being interviewed about what she was looking for in a man. She was single and the person interviewing her asked "What are you looking for in a husband?" Her response was "I don't want someone who smokes, I don't want someone who doesn't have a job, I don't want someone who doesn't love children, I don't want someone who is a momma's boy, I don't want someone who is not faithful." This woman ran down a list of all the things she didn't want. It's no surprise she was single. Her focus was on all the things she didn't want. If the right guy came along she wouldn't recognize the qualities he had that she wanted because her focus and energy was on all the things she didn't want.

Another ill-fated fact about limiting beliefs is that they program your mind. We are always talking about thinking differently and how our thoughts determine our actions and behaviors. When you are consistently thinking about and talking about what you are not, your mind will prove you are right.

Here is another tidbit you may not have known. It has been scientifically proven that your mind does not comprehend the word "don't." When the woman was talking about what she wanted in a husband she was saying things like "I don't want someone who smokes" and all her mind heard was "I want someone who smokes."

How many of you remember being young in the summer time and ready to go outside to play with your friends. Just as you are running out the door your mother or grandmother yells out "Don't slam my door." The first thing you do is slam her door? All your mind heard was "slam the door."

Where your focus goes, your energy flows. In the Bible in the Book of Job, Job says "What I have feared has come upon me; what I dreaded has happened to me." If your focus and attention is on what you fear and what you don't want, you give your mind no choice but to prove yourself right and bring all those things to pass. Your mind has two parts, the thinker and the prover. Whatever the thinker thinks it is the job of the prover to prove the thinker right!

We are constantly fighting. And the biggest fight we will ever have will be in our own mind. Your words are powerful and can change the world (or at least your view of it.) So, I encourage you to **FIGHT**! Fight for your abilities, fight for your potential, fight for your goals, and fight for your dreams.

What Now

1. Be aware of what you say to yourself.
2. Consciously listen to the words you use.
3. Remove Don't from your self-talk
4. Focus on what you want, and not what you don't want
5. Understand that what you focus on will grow
6. If you fight for your limitations, you get to keep them.

6

I Quit

Quitting is a secret to success most people overlook!

Based on how we have been programmed, we usually think of quitting as what losers do. There is a strong negative connotation around the word "Quit." Society is constantly telling us to never quit, especially in the realm of being successful. Ironically, quitting may be that surreptitious action that may catapult you to a level of incredible success.

How you perceive quitting may be the very thing that is holding you back from achieving what you desire. The mental association you have established with the concept of quitting may need to be reframed. The belief you have about quitting should be challenged.

Quitting can be a powerful action. Used properly, it can give you the ability to achieve a higher level of success. It has the capability of moving you from good to great. This one action can help streamline your process of having success.

Does this take courage? Yes, it takes intestinal fortitude to recognize something that you have become accustom to doing and decide to stop. When certain actions become part of who you are, your brain simulates pain when you think of no longer performing those actions. This is why it is such a challenge for most people to quit a bad habit. It is easier for them to continue down the same path, and participate in the same activities, than to abruptly turn and go in another direction.

In order to quit anything, you must acknowledge fear. The fear that all the hard work, blood, sweat and tears that you put into that project, job, relationship, or other commitment can be viewed as a waste. That feeling can be terrifying. No one wants to feel like they have wasted their time. And no one wants to be labeled and recognized as a Quitter. That fear, of being a quitter, is more painful to most than the action of quitting. Fear of quitting should never be a factor in making the right decisions for yourself.

When you invest your time, energy and money into something, you expect the outcome you imagined when you first started. Quitting can mean not seeing that outcome come to fruition. This often holds people back, even when they know the goal or idea has run its course. We're so loss-averse that we will suffer through what we no longer want or need because we put up our time and money.

This is what economists call the "sunk-cost fallacy." This is the belief that you can't quit because of all the time or money you invested. The idea doesn't consider that you have received what you need from the endeavor. What this focuses on is that your money and time are more important than your happiness and achievement of your ultimate goal.

Several years ago, I started a business as an independent representative for a worldwide product company. My wife and I loved their products. One of the factors in our decision to start the business was that we saw a way to earn some great income. To make money in this venture, we had to first make an investment - our money and our time. Success wasn't something that was going to happen overnight. Understanding that, we jumped in with both feet.

We began to build our business. We put a significant amount of energy into this endeavor. We also began to put time into our own personal development. As time went on I started to feel that I was being called to do something else with my life.

The more I learned and the more I was open and honest with myself I realized the business wasn't my calling or mission. After fighting this for a while and my wife believing my path was in a different direction, I decided to change my focus and move in the direction of what I believed was my mission in life. So, what does this all mean? It means...I Quit!

Yep, I Quit. I quit running that business. I turned and looked for a way to move forward with my passion. There may come a time when you are to follow a path just long enough to learn something or get where you need to be to move towards your true passion. For me I learned valuable lessons that I don't think I would have learned if I had not started that business. There were people who made deposits in my life and helped to change my way of thinking.

Leaving the business was a tough decision initially, but it was the right decision.

When you find yourself in these types of challenging situations, it doesn't mean you are quitting on your dream. You must be honest with yourself and ask if you are on the right path and if you have learned the lessons you needed to learn in that space and time.

Remember, you and I have been taught and conditioned to believe that quitting is synonymous with failure. I never looked at quitting that business as a failure. How can something that taught you lessons to assist you in growing and understanding your passion be considered a failure?

Turning away from something that you are doing, without achieving what most people would consider success, is looked upon as quitting. As an entrepreneur, or just someone with something to achieve, I always heard quotes and sayings about quitting like this:

- Quitters never win, and winners never quit
- Quitting is not an option
- The only way to fail is to quit

When this is your concept of quitting you feel that you can't stop something that you started, even when your heart is no longer in it.

Deciding to quit or to stick it out is a great quandary of life. This takes an introspective look inside yourself. Today's society has ingrained in our culture that you should not quit something that you have started. You should keep pushing through. Keep grinding, even when your inner voice tells you that you should not be doing it. This is the point when you need to challenge your belief about quitting.

Let me be clear, just because something is challenging and is not happening as quickly as you would like, doesn't mean that you should quit. Achieving your mission and goals in life will take time and effort. You must be prepared to work hard, have set backs, be disappointed and maybe even start over. The only reason that we contemplate our decision during these times is that we have a misconception that it should be easy. Somehow the idea that if it doesn't work on the first try or happen how we imagined, it's something that was not meant for us. This is part of our paradigm programming that is not true and needs to be re-programmed.

If you take a moment and think about it, as you grow you quit things all the time. The natural process of growth requires that you leave certain actions and activities behind during your journey. This includes things that you may have enjoyed, but you have outgrown. Most people hate to let go so they have that box of trinkets, in the basement or attic, that remind them of the things they once loved but no longer serve them. All the old trophies, teddy bears, games and pictures you kept, that remind you of the activities you invested in but have since quit.

Instead of looking at it as quitting, you need to reframe how you interpret the idea of moving forward. A better way to frame it is to look at it as pivoting. You have developed a vision for what you want to accomplish in your life. As you travel on your journey you will come to a point where you have to make a change and turn in a new direction to reach the goal. At that turning point you will leave things behind, things that you must quit.

When you reach these turning points in your growth your priorities will change. At this point you must re-evaluate your actions and change those that are not in alignment with your priorities.

Here is the key to quitting, you must know what, why and when you need to quit. Quitting should not be a random act. This is not something you should do just because your goal is challenging, or other people are telling you that it is not something you should do.

Consider these key points when contemplating quitting anything.

1. **What should you quit?** - When you now think about quitting, you must account for the actions and activities you are investing your time in. If you find that there are activities that you are participating in that no longer serve you, contribute to damaging your health, pry at good relationships or no longer move you toward your goal, it is time to quit those activities.
2. **Why should you quit?** - You should quit if what you are doing is not getting you closer to what you want to accomplish in life. If you are hurting others in the process. If what you are doing is what others believe you should do and it's not your passion. Also, consider quitting if your decision to continue is based on fear, a sense of responsibility or you don't want to admit you made a bad choice.

3. **When should you quit?** - You should quit when you gain awareness that something you are doing aligns with What You Should Quit and Why You Should Quit. This, I know, is easier said than done. Quitting can be a process. I don't suggest that you just up and quit your job because you don't like it anymore. When you quit it is a good idea to have a plan.

7

The "How" Doesn't Matter if...

Impossible is a matter of believe, not a matter of fact.

When I began to understand this concept, it was, like Oprah says, an Aha moment for me. The light bulb turned on and things began to become much clearer. The reason why I wasn't accomplishing the things I said I wanted in life, why I wasn't becoming the person I wanted to be, started to make sense.

Before we talk about the "IF", because if you are like most people, you paid little attention to the rest of that statement and just jumped to asking yourself "What is the IF, IF WHAT." Let's first talk about the "HOW." The "HOW," this is the process needed to accomplish something. What are the necessary steps for you to achieve that thing you want in life?

To become a business owner there are things you need to do, to become a better spouse there are things you need to do, to get a new car there are things you need to do, to overcome an addiction there are things you need to do, to have children there are things you need to do, to pay off your bills there are things you need to do. I'm sure you have many things that you would love to do or achieve. Whatever those things are, there are steps you need to take to accomplish or acquire them. That is the "HOW." How do I get it done?

The "HOW" may mean you need to learn some new skills. Or, you may need to use skills that you already possess. If there are new skills you need to learn there are many resources available for you to learn the "HOW." YouTube, Google, Books, Seminars, Mentors, there are many of ways to learn the "HOW."

But none of that will mean anything "IF…" (here it comes get ready, brace yourself) "The HOW doesn't matter IF…you don't believe! How many times have you done something you didn't believe in or believed you could do? No matter how many books you read or how many seminars you go to or how many times you go back to school, none of these things will matter or help you achieve your goal IF you don't BELIEVE you can do it or deserve it.

You may want that new job, or the promotion with the corner office and the rubber tree plant, an amazing spouse that spoils you rotten, the big house on the hill with the cars and boat and breath-taking vacations, you may "WANT" all of those things. But it may seem farfetched, so you tell yourself "I have to be realistic." At that moment your dream dies. Being realistic is a death penalty for your belief.

Understand this; *"Being realistic is the most commonly traveled road to mediocrity."* What is your reality? Everybody's reality is different. Your reality is based on your perception, your perception of who you think you are, your environment, and what you believe you are capable of accomplishing. If the people that are close to you don't have the corner office or the big house or the nice car or the loving and growing relationship, then your perception will become one of, maybe I can't have my dream because I don't know anyone who has anything like that. If you look at your bank account and the number you see doesn't have any commas in it, or maybe it's not even 3 digits, you may perceive that you can't take that dream vacation or pay off your bills.

Your perception can be misleading. This can produce a false reality, or should I say, "an alternative reality." How you see your current situation should not be a dictator of your future. Where you are in life at this moment is temporary. Resist creating a vision of your future solely on this moment. In other words, you shouldn't make a permanent decision based on a temporary situation.

In the early 1970's Bill Gates said, "There will be a computer in every home." At the time computers were these humongous machines, they were slow and very expensive. No one believed him. They thought he was crazy. If he based his belief on the perception of others, we probably wouldn't use computers the way we do today. Bill Gates believed and then he figured out the HOW.

We need to take the same approach, believe and then figure out the HOW. Too often the opposite is done. We go out and spend money, time and resources trying to figure out the HOW. Yet, in our mind, we haven't solidified our belief in what is actually possible. We go about it with the mindset that if I learn all this stuff or do what people "say" I need to do, I will get what I want.

When my youngest son was 10 years old, he played basketball for the boys and girls club in our area. That was his first year playing County basketball. Several years before this, I put up a basketball court in our driveway and he would go out there often to shoot around. I would go out there with him to teach him how to shoot a jump shot, layups and show him some dribbling techniques to help him increase his skill level and confidence. I even bought him a video training program to teach him proper shooting form and dribbling skills.

He would go outside and practice often. Now he's on his first County basketball team and it's time to use his skills. They are ready to play their first game. The game starts and he's on the court. His teammate passes him the ball. He is wide open, and he freezes like he's doing the mannequin challenge. I'm screaming, from the stands, shoot, shoot. He passes the ball as quickly as he can. He didn't take one shot that first game.

Why? He practiced all the time. He watched the videos I bought him. What happened? My son knew how to shoot. He practiced consistently, but when he got in that game, he didn't Believe he could score. The "HOW" didn't matter, because he didn't believe.

You may be familiar with the saying "one ounce of doubt and you're out." No matter how much you study or practice, if you have just one ounce of doubt, you will not achieve your goal. Instead, you will sabotage yourself. You

The How Doesn't Matter If...

will unconsciously create situations that move you away from your goal.

Your brain was designed to protect you. It will create these situations to keep you safe. When you don't believe, and you are trying to accomplish something your brain interprets that as fear. If it senses fear it activates your amygdala, which controls your brains fight, flight or freeze mode. This also initiates the shutdown of your pre-frontal cortex, which controls your higher-level thinking.

Knowing "How" to do something is not enough. You must also "Believe" that you can do it. If you are not moving toward accomplishing what you desire, take some time and honestly answer the question: "Do you believe that you can?"

Once you build belief, then learning the process of "HOW" will become easier and more enjoyable. The HOW doesn't matter if you don't Believe. Build your belief in yourself and what you want to achieve.

What Now

1. **Remove the word IMPOSSIBLE from your vocabulary.** Impossible is a limiting belief and what you are really saying is that I don't believe I can do it. If you think about it, you are probably just like Bill Gates, looking at doing something that you never been done before. So, you have to believe that what you want to do is possible, you just must believe that YOU can do it. Once you tell your brain that it is possible you have given it the

command to start looking for ways to make it happen.
2. **Be careful what Thoughts you attach emotions to.** When you attach an emotion to a thought you begin to create a belief. Those beliefs dictate your actions and those actions become your life. My son had the thought that he was not as good as the other kids and attached the emotion of fear to that thought and it began to create his belief. If he had the thought that he could make his shots and attached the emotion of happiness he would have created the belief that he could score, and he would have shot the ball that first game.
3. **Create small victories.** Your belief level will increase if you have small successes. I worked with my son to get him to shoot a layup in his next game. His opportunity came and he took the shot, he made it. So now he had a small victory. He made a shot in a real game. This helped increase his belief. This also gave him the confidence to take more shots. In their fourth game, they were down by one point late in the 4th quarter. My son got fouled shooting a 3 pointer. He didn't make the shot, but he was getting 3 foul shots. They are down by one point it's 3.5 seconds left in the game. He steps to the foul line, takes a deep breath shoots and makes the first foul shot. Now the game is tied. Worst case scenario…we go into overtime. He shoots and makes the second foul shoot, now they are winning. And then he shoots the 3rd and final foul shot…he makes it. Now his team is up by 2 points with 3.5 seconds left in the game. His team doesn't allow the other team to get off a shot and they win…He is the hero. All because he started to belief he could.

4. **Create positive "I AM" statements.** These statements help to program or reprogram your unconscious mind about who you are and what you are capable of doing. Repeat them to yourself several times a day. Read them and speak them out loud. As you continue to repeat these statements and accept them as true you will begin to believe them and your actions will now flow with your new beliefs. (Chapter 9 discusses the I AM statement in more detail.)

8
The Equation That Changes Everything

"You can't stop the waves from coming but you can learn how to surf." Jon Kabat-Zinn

Jack Canfield, author of "The Success Principles, How to Get from Where You Are to Where You Want to Be," shared an equation he learned that I believe changes everything.

The equation is: **E+R=O. Event + Response = Outcome**.

Things are going to happen in your life, and when they do, what is your response going to be? There are people who will make excuses and blame certain events that have happened in their life as to why they are not where they want to be. Here is what you must understand, it is not just "What" has happened to you that determines where you are in life, but "How you respond" to the "What" that really matters.

Events will always occur and most of the time you will have no control over those events. But, you will ALWAYS have control over your RESPONSE. Based on that response, you will dictate the outcome.

Let me repeat this fact again: In life, we all have events that will happen. The outcomes of these events can determine the life you live. These events can be interpreted as negative or positive, based on your perspective. Events can be a feeling that you experience, a comment someone makes, rush hour traffic, illness, wellness, the weather, death of a loved one, a promotion on your job, and so on.

We experience numerous events that we consider minor and label them "just a part of life." When these small events occur, we usually don't pay much attention to their significance, because they happen so often. Then there are events that we label "major" and allow to have a huge impact on our life. Everyone creates their own labels and they attach them to events based on what they have experienced in the past. These past experiences create a cognitive map in your brain built upon how you interpreted or labeled prior experiences. How an event is labeled is based on your thoughts and beliefs about yourself and your world around you.

When an event happens and there are undesired results, many believe someone outside of themselves is responsible. They believe it is the fault of the President, the government, their boss, a car accident, the loss of their job, their parents, their spouse, anyone but themselves. This thinking is why, I believe, so many never experience significant personal success. They have been conditioned to believe that they are entitled to a great life and someone owes them. The belief is, what has happened to them is due to the events that have occurred in their life.

Is it truly the events that are holding your back from your greatness? If so, how do you explain the hundreds, if not thousands, of people who have overcome similar events? Truth is, these factors do exist, but if success was based solely on these events no one would be successful.

A couple had twin boys. The father was an alcoholic and abusive. He would drink often and mentally and physically abuse the boys and their mother. This went on for years.

When the twins grew up they were interviewed and asked about their childhood and their life as adults. The first brother interviewed said he was an alcoholic and had become abusive to his family. When asked why he thought he became an alcoholic his reply was, "my father was an alcoholic, that's what I saw growing up, what was I supposed to be?"

Then the other brother was interviewed. He was asked about his life as an adult. His response was, "I have a successful career and a beautiful family and I have never had a drink of alcohol." When asked why he thought he became so successful and never had a drink he said, "My father was an alcoholic and abusive, that's what I saw growing up, what was I supposed to be?"

If their father being abusive and an alcoholic (the *event*) was the deciding factor, they both should have been alcoholics and abusive (the *outcome*.) But as we learned, they weren't. Their individual response to the event determined the outcomes they experienced.

What's missing from the equation for most people is their response. How do you respond when an event occurs? A better question may be, do you respond or do you react? Majority of individuals have an immediate reaction when they experience an event in life.

This knee-jerk reaction is the brain being lazy. Your brain is always looking for short cuts, ways to reduce the amount of energy it uses. To aid in this process we create habits and patterns. Habits allow the brain to react, and this drastically reduces the need to consciously think.

When an event occurs, your brain looks for past events and how you once reacted and reacts the same way. This is another example of functioning on "autopilot." This is part of the reason why you may find yourself repeating the same type of events and getting the same outcomes throughout your life. If you react this way you may find yourself dating the same type of person or working the same type of jobs even though you *say* that's not what you want in your life.

Let's be clear, there are times when you need your brain to operate in this capacity. If a bus is heading straight for you, you need your brain to react and get you out of the way.

But, the determining factor in your success or failure is not the external conditions and circumstances. When an event happens, most people evaluate the outcome. If the outcome is not one they want, unconsciously they create a thought. This thought becomes attached to the emotions that they are feeling at the time of the event. In turn, a new limiting belief is created.

When you have limiting beliefs, you evoke negative emotions and engage in self-defeating behaviors. In this state, you probably complain, blame and deflect. If this is the mindset you default to when an event happens, you must accept the outcomes that you have in life.

In order to experience different outcomes, you must approach life events differently. The equation that changes everything says, "**the event + your response = the outcome**." You will have little to no control over most events. But you will always have 100% control over how you respond.

Moving forward, when an event happens your goal should be to respond, not react. This will require that you change your thinking. At the time of the event you must consciously turn off autopilot. You may have to take a moment, pause and breathe. Regain control over your thoughts and decide what you want the outcome to be.

People who have had success have learned how to change their responses. They realize that they have a choice in every situation, and so do you. This may be a challenge for you, especially in the beginning. To help make this mind shift less daunting, just know you have the freedom to choose how you respond.

Your response has three components - your thoughts, your emotions and your behavior. The order in which you engage these components does play a big part in your response. Often people think of change and look at their behavior before they get their thoughts in order. You also must understand your emotional triggers to know how you typically respond to certain events.

If you are looking to lose weight your primary focus should not be how you eat, what you eat and how much you eat.

These are your eating behaviors. This will only give you a temporary loss, if any. Your thoughts and emotions will take over your behaviors. But, if you understand the emotional trigger that makes you overeat you are better prepared to identify when those events happen. You also need to be aware of how you think about food. Do you eat to live or do you live to eat? After you understand what triggers your emotions to eat and how you think about eating, then you can focus on modifying your eating behaviors. This will give you greater long-term success.

Changing your response to events will require you to be deliberate and conscious of your thoughts, emotions and behaviors. As you start down this path, old thoughts and beliefs will tempt you. The brain will want to react how it has always reacted (remember the cognitive roadmap.) You are creating new habits and this may take time and effort. But, rest assured, once you have reprogrammed how you view events that happen and your response, you will begin to have the outcomes you desire.

What Now

When an event happens in your life remember the following steps.

1. Identify the event.
2. Realize you have choices.
3. Pause and think about what you want as an outcome.
4. Create a response that coincides with your desired outcome.

9

The Great *"I AM"*

"Any time you start a sentence with I AM you are creating what you are and what you want to be"
Dr. Wayne Dyer

I AM! These are two of the most powerful words you can say to yourself. These two words are part of the programming process of our unconscious mind. Whatever follows these words in a statement is what your mind will begin to manifest.

Do you say things like:

- I am so busy.
- I am broke.
- I am tired.
- I am working a job I hate.
- I am overwhelmed.
- I am in debt.
- I am fat.

- I am not good at this.

Statements like these, repeated over time, usually take your life in just that direction. If said enough with conviction, our brain will believe what is being said. Once you believe something, it becomes a part of you and the belief will become manifest. You then begin to take actions based on those beliefs.

You are always right! Anything that you say or think your brain MUST prove to be correct. Here is how one of my mentors, George Zalucki, put it, "The mind has two parts, the Thinker and the Prover. It is the job of the Thinker to Think and the job of the Prover to Prove what the Thinker Thought."

I'm sure you may have heard the saying "thoughts are things." These things, that thoughts become, are paramount to what you get in life. Creating desired outcomes come from paying attention to what you think.

The words that follow "I am" do not have to be negative. "I am" statements can be used to serve you.

- I am feeling phenomenal. (my personal favorite)
- I am getting better every day.
- I am doing the things I love.
- I am managing my money so all my bills are paid on time.
- I am working a job that is giving me the opportunity to move ahead.
- I am paying off everyone I owe.
- I am finding ways to keep my mind positively occupied.

Positive "I am" statements, or what some call affirmations, help reprogram your unconscious mind. The key is, being aware that what you say is more than just words. You are, more than likely, using "I am" statements more than you know.

I have four kids. One of my goals as a parent is to help them become conscious of their thoughts and what they say. Whenever one of my children say the phrase "I am hungry," my reply is always "I am Darius, nice to meet you Hungry." When I respond to them I hold out my hand to shake theirs as if we are meeting for the first time. As they were growing up and even to this day, I do this every time I hear them say "I am hungry."

This story about my kids saying, "I am hungry," may seem trivial and small. But we are consistently using these types of phrases without a second thought, not knowing we are programming our minds. I do this with my kids so that they start to become aware of what they are actually saying, and to annoy them sometimes. On a daily basis, we program ourselves without any knowledge of what is happening.

This programming determines how or if we see opportunities that will get us where we want to go in life. My kids have learned how to reframe their statement of being hungry. Now they will say things like, "I need some food", or "can we get something to eat."

Think about some of your I AM statements? You may have to slow down and think about what you are saying. You may go through your day making statements unaware of the power you speak. How many times have you said, out loud or to yourself, I am not good at something? Or maybe you have said "I am not having a good day." These types of comments have, unfortunately, become common place in our society.

If everyone around you uses statements like these, you may not think much of it when you use them. But, the truth is, if you want to level up in life you have to change your internal conversation. This is where you must be honest about where you are in your life and understand that how you are programming your mind plays a part in your results.

To move forward, you have to be aware of what you are saying. If you are using I am statements that don't serve you, you must interrupt that process. When you notice you are using statements that are not positive and uplifting, you need to challenge those thoughts. You can't move forward and WISH yourself into your ultimate situation and fail to realize that it all starts with your thinking.

Here are 3 steps to interrupting this process:

Step 1: Start paying attention to what you are saying to yourself.

What do the conversations you have with yourself sound like? Are you using negative I am statements?

You mind is constantly taking selfies. A picture of what your world looks like in your own mind. When you have thoughts, you need to understand that this is your inside picture of your world. This is who you are at that time. We all have an inside picture of what the world looks like. This is the mental image of yourself, your surroundings and your circumstances. Your inside picture is so powerful because your outside picture (what is actually happening in your world) must match your inside picture. If it doesn't, your mind will work hard to make sure your outside picture matches your inside picture. It will not try to make your inside picture match your outside picture.

It is impossible to think one way and have certain beliefs in your mind and your outside world not represent those thoughts and beliefs. So again, the first step in interrupting this process is to Start paying attention to what you are saying to yourself.

Step 2: Decide to change.

Make a decision, that you are going to change your thoughts. Decide you are going to reprogram your mind if you are not moving in the direction that you ultimately want to go in your life.

Here's one tip that helped me tremendously when I decided to implement this step. When I caught myself saying or thinking something that wasn't in sync with what I wanted out of my life, I would ask myself "Is this a message I want to match?" Remember, your inside picture must match your outside picture.

Step 3: Install some new programming.

Reprogram your unconscious mind. You may be asking "How do I do that?" The answer is something I'm sure most of you have heard before, affirmations, incantations, declarations, or mantras. A short positive phrase depicting a desired outcome.

We may have all heard of them before, and maybe even tried them. But the truth is most people don't create them properly and/or they are not consistent with them. An affirmation can be life changing.

There are two main reasons why you would use an affirmation:

1. Affirmations keep your mind occupied with positive information. Even though you may think you can, you cannot think two thoughts at the same time. And if your mind is occupied with positive thoughts that's less time you have to think negative thoughts.

2. Affirmations reprogram your unconscious mind. 95% of what we do daily, we do unconsciously. This reprogramming is done the same way your mind was programmed in the first place, repetition and emotion. An affirmation must be repeated consistently and there must be strong (positive) emotion tied to the thought. A thought tied to emotions creates a belief.

Why do affirmations work? It's science. Yep, science. An affirmation created with what I will call "perfect language" is in line with how your mind works. Your unconscious mind can't distinguish between what is real and what's imagined. That's the good news and the bad news. This means that every thought that you have is taken as fact.

When you use affirmations, you are not changing how your mind works, you are working within the natural tendencies of your mind.

You may not realize it, but you are repeating affirmations all the time. When you say, "I am," you are programming your mind. That programming can be positive or negative.

We need to create affirmations that work with how our brain functions. These statements must be repeated several times a day, in order for them to effectively change our unconscious mind. Affirmations, or I am statements, help guide you to the outcomes you want in life.

――――――――――  ――――――――

Here are 8 basic guidelines for creating your perfect language affirmations:

1. Start with the words "I AM." These are the two most powerful words.
2. Use the present tense. Make your statement as though it is already happening.
3. Make your statement in the positive. Affirm what you want, not what you don't want.
4. Keep it brief.
5. Make it specific.
6. Include an action word ending with – ing.
7. Make your statement believable but stretch yourself.
8. Include at least one dynamic emotion or feeling word. It should create a positive emotional impact. (Use words like – "excited" "powerful" "phenomenal")

10

Be Curious

"I have no special talents. I am only passionately curious." Albert Einstein

We are born curious. As children this is how we grow and learn. To infants and toddlers, everything is new. They are eager to understand their surroundings and themselves. During this time in life, the brain is extremely malleable. There are new experiences happening every day.

When an infant sees a toy or object that it has never seen before it has a huge desire to figure the object out. They are curious. They pick up the object, they put it in their mouth, they shake it, they want to know what it can do and what they can do with it. This is the beginning stage of learning.

As a child grows and develops they begin to speak. This becomes an incredible new tool that allows them to expand their curiosity. Now they have the ability to learn from others, by asking questions. They are no longer left to their own experiences to learn.

It is unfortunate that parents, who are not aware of the effects curiosity has on a developing brain, either stop answering their child's questions or hush them so they don't even ask questions any more. There are parents, guardians and teachers that become annoyed with hearing the question "Why?" Children, on average, ask from 25 to 50 questions an hour. But, after being told to stop asking so many questions this number diminishes tremendously.

After a few years of this, the child has unconsciously learned that they should not ask questions or explore the unknown. And if they do, they are more than likely met with discouragement. This young impressionable being, now in school, rarely asks a question or challenges their thoughts or beliefs. Their answers become more valued than their questions and inquisitive thoughts. That same child now asks on average, about 2-5 questions an hour.

If this was your situation growing up, as an adult, you probably don't ask many questions. You may feel more comfortable answering questions as opposed to asking them. Thus, preparing you for college entrance exams and job interviews. This is the industrial era way of learning. A time when you had your curiosity smothered, so you couldn't challenge the status quo.

If you don't feel you are a curious person, you may be someone who had their curiosity smothered. I want to challenge you to allow your curious mind to resurface. This is not a childish trait that should be forgotten about after adolescence. Research has shown curiosity to be associated with higher levels of positive emotions, lower levels of anxiety, more satisfaction with life, and greater psychological well-being.

Regaining your sense of curiosity is vital if you want to have success in today's world. Being curious energizes you to go out and seek information. Your curiosity pulls you toward the answers you are seeking. Curiosity sparks the part of the brain called the dopaminergic system or the brains wanting system. Once curiosity is elicited it increases activity in the midbrain and the nucleus accumbens, the "reward circuit" of the brain.

Developing your natural curiosity, simply, makes you feel good. Your brain rewards you when you search and discover answers, by releasing dopamine. This gives you a natural high. *Neuron* magazine published a study which suggested that as we become curious, our brain's chemistry changes and helps us to retain information and increases our learning.

I wrote this book because I was curious. When I was in my early twenties, I was introduced to personal development. A mentor at the time forced me to listen to these cassette tapes (I know I'm dating myself) of people talking. In the beginning I didn't get it. I wanted to listen to music when I was in my car, not someone talking, trying to get me all pumped up. I vividly remember asking my mentor, "how long do I *have to* listen to these tapes?" He replied calmly, "until you *want to*, then you don't *have to* anymore." Then one day I was driving to work and it clicked. Someone on one of those tapes said something that piqued my curiosity.

Once I finished listening to that tape I wanted to listen to the next one. And before I knew, I was hooked. I fell in love with the teachings of people like Jim Rohn, Zig Ziglar, Tony Robbins, Les Brown, Jack Canfield and the likes. They had me hanging on to every word they said. I couldn't wait to get in my car and drive so I could listen to them speak to me. That was the moment when I *wanted to* listen to the tapes and I didn't feel like I was being forced.

Unbeknownst to me at the time, my brain was releasing dopamine and rewarding me for listening. When I would get to my destination I would get out of my car feeling like I could conquer the world. This feeling made me want to learn more.

Being curious is simply the desire to know more. And that is exactly what I wanted. From the moment I listened to that first tape to now, I have listened to thousands of hours of audio, read hundreds of books and attended countless seminars to continue to learn and grow.

My initial curiosity led me to study success principles, mindset, leadership, neuroscience and how to become a thought-provoking speaker. From that, my mind created the idea of writing a book. And now you hold in your hands the byproduct of my curiosity.

Being brilliant starts with being curious. The majority of brilliant minds in history and today were curious. They were fueled by the desire to know more. Many of the best innovations are results of curiosity. They were much like that small child that wanted to know "why?"

There are many additional benefits of being curious besides learning new things. As I think about listening to those tapes a few come to mind.

Being curious:
- Drives you to seek more knowledge. You will not be satisfied with how things appear on the surface. This drive will push you to delve deeper.
- Keeps you thinking about creative possibilities. Your mind will stay active. This is important because your brain is a muscle and it gets stronger with continued exercise. Thinking and seeking answers is a form of brain exercise.
- Increases dopamine in your system. This helps you become more focused, productive and motivated.
- Makes you a better listener. You grow personally when you are genuinely interested in others. You will begin to pay more attention to what is being said because you have a desire to learn.
- Helps you to be happier, calmer and lowers your anxiety levels. This creates a more positive outlook on life.
- Increases your intelligence and learning. Studies have shown that if you are curious about a topic you will tend to pick it up faster. Curiosity has been shown to help "prime" the brain for learning.
- Helps you to see new worlds of possibilities. If you have a curious mind it will seek out new opportunities.

There are many benefits to being curious. And at the same time, curiosity can also be used to numb your brain. This is based on why you initiate your curious mind. If you are curious about something because you are afraid of what you will miss out on or you feel you will be left behind, this can be a distraction to you achieving your goals.

A few examples of mind numbing curiosity are binge watching TV show series, constantly checking your

Facebook timeline, seeing what your "friends" are up to right now, seeking approval, likes and wanting to feel good all the time and getting trapped in the paradox of choice. These are just a few ways being curious can be useless.

Something else to be aware of, if you lose curiosity, you may start to make assumptions and jump to conclusions. Asking questions and seeking information helps you to broaden your perspective about others and the world around you. Understanding this enables you to be more empathetic. Conscious curiosity helps you imagine the possibilities, what someone else may be thinking and helps you feel what they may feel.

So, be curious my friend! It can literally change your brain. Curiosity is a habit you must nurture. It takes focus to use curiosity to benefit you and not get caught in brain numbing activities. Remember, most children have been programmed to not be curious. This creates adults who don't ask questions, are content with the status quo and never find their true passion.

What Now

Here are a few tips to increase your sense of curiosity:

1. **Be open**. Allow yourself to let in new ideas and thoughts. Assume nothing. Notice what you may have never noticed. Give yourself permission to try something new.
2. **Ask questions**. Every question can have merit and there literally are no stupid questions. Each question can lead to bigger more revealing questions.

3. **Become comfortable outside of your comfort zone.** Curiosity will push you to learn new things. Diversify what you read, listen to and watch. New experiences will keep your mind active.
4. **Dig deeper.** Go beyond the surface. Look to find the benefit and positive in every situation.
5. **Say Yes.** Accept the challenge. Discover alternative ways to accomplish the same task. Explore the possibilities.

11

What Did You Expect?

"Nobody succeeds beyond his or her wildest expectations unless he or she begins with some wild expectations."
Ralph Charell

In life, you get what you expect with certainty. And you only get what you expect. The reason for this is because you act upon your expectations, not what you want. What you want and what you expect are two very different things. It is possible, and even common, to want one thing and to expect the opposite.

Expectations are the list of thoughts you build up that tell you how things should be. They typically keep you feeling safe and they can propel or prevent you from being fully present in your life and living to your highest potential. Your reality is determined by your expectations, more than anything else in life. If you want to be rich, but you expect you will be poor, you will be poor.

So often, people believe that they are making decisions and acting upon what they want. The reality is that their thoughts, words and actions are based on their expectations. Consciously they say, "I want to achieve this goal", but unconsciously their mind creates stories that tell them they can't achieve the goal. Regardless of what you consciously say, if your unconscious expectation doesn't match, your autopilot will kick in and you will follow your unconscious expectations.

If you are not aware of this process, it can cause you to become frustrated, angry or even quit striving to achieve. You may have been here before. Maybe you wanted to lose 10 pounds. You said you wanted to do it and you begin down the path you think will get you to your goal. A few days in or maybe a few weeks into your journey you find that you are not getting the results you desired. Is it because exercise and eating right doesn't work? Or is it that you are unconsciously believing that you are the person you see in the mirror?

When you set a goal and feel like you are not moving in the right direction, you need to disrupt your thinking. This disruption requires you to become aware of what is going on in your head. You must identify, what I call your **E.T.A**. Your **Emotions**, **Thoughts** and **Actions**.

Here is how it plays out. You set a goal to lose weight. Your **Emotion** is you feel worried that if you don't lose weight your body will become diseased, no one will love you and you will die before you should. Next you have the **Thoughts** that you have been overweight all your life and food has always been your comfort when things didn't go how you wanted. Your **Actions**, doubting that can do it, you start multiple crazy diets and going to the gym everyday putting unnecessary stress on yourself looking for results overnight, then you binge eat when you haven't lost any weight.

It is detrimental to your success, to work toward one thing and expect something different. If your goal is to lose 10 pounds and your unconscious mind believes that you are supposed to be a big person, if you don't change your E.T.A. you will remain a big person. Even if you lose the weight, you more than likely, will gain it back if you don't disrupt your unconscious expectation. You will work toward your goal, but secretly sabotage yourself.

You have an unconscious expectation of yourself and your life. This is the belief of who you are, what you look like, what you know and what you can do. If you lose weight and your unconscious mind doesn't recognize the person you have become, it will work to get you back to who it recognizes. This expectation not only determines what you have and accomplish, but it also establishes what you will settle for in life.

When I was in my early thirties, I was laid off (fancy word for fired) from my job. This became, what I considered at the time, a rough period in my life. I went from making $50,000 a year to making nothing overnight. At the time, I was working as a software trainer and never had much of a problem getting a job. This time was different. I was laid off on September 10, 2001, the day before the 9/11 attacks on the United States. This was significant because after the attacks very few companies were hiring, especially software trainers.

Looking back over this time, I realize my unconscious expectation was that if I didn't have a job I could not make money. If I didn't make money I couldn't support myself and my family. I had no luck finding a company looking to hire a trainer and what little money I had saved was dwindling quickly. The only job offer I had was as a security guard at a hotel making minimum wage. The hours were from midnight to 8am. I took the job and I hated it, but believed I had no other choice.

I now understand that believing I had no other choice came from my unconscious expectations, allowing me to settle for this position. When your mind creates an expectation, it is based on the belief of whether or not you can achieve what you say you want. I became a believer! I started to believe that I wasn't worth more than a minimum wage, graveyard shift, rent-a-cop security job. (No disrespect to those who work as security guards, we need you.)

How does your brain create these expectations? There are three key factors that help in establishing your expectations:

- Your Imagination
- Other people around you
- Your past experiences

When I first lost my job and realized that companies were hesitant to hire, I began imagining my life without being a software trainer and having a job in that field. These thoughts began to multiply quickly. What started out as the thought of "I will not have a problem getting another job," turned into thoughts of living with my parents forever because I wouldn't be able to afford my own home. My imagination was running wild with all sorts of negative thoughts and outcomes for my life.

My friends and family that cared about me and loved me, initially told me that everything would be all right. Then their words began to change. The conversations evolved into, "you just need a job, take whatever you are offered." In subtle ways, they would point out to me that sending out my resume to every training company I could was not working. They were not directly negative to me but looking back the core of their message was "just give up on being a trainer right now." Hearing these types of messages, along with my thoughts and imagination of my "future", I started to sink into the "reality" of my life.

After a short period of time, the successes I had in my past faded away and were overrun with the "new" reality of my life. The new experiences that I was having were of being rejected, turned away and ignored. I was becoming dependent on others, like my parents, to just survive. I was the father of a young son and I was not able to provide for him like he deserved. He was indirectly suffering because of the expectations I was creating for my life.

We are not typically taught to spend time exploring our expectations. Rarely, are we encouraged to consider alternatives to what we have experienced and been told throughout our life. If you don't give the proper attention to your expectations, their effects will have an impression of permanence and inevitability on your life.

As I went through this brief period in my life, it felt like it would always be that way. For a moment, I couldn't see the proverbial "light at the end of the tunnel." My expectations blinded me from seeing what else was possible. I had created mental filters that prohibited me from seeing beyond my current situation.

Our thoughts are like magnetics that attract things like themselves. Take time to inventory your life. Examine and question your expectations. There is a correlation between what you think and what you experience. Your brain works by anticipating. It is constantly predicting what it thinks is likely to happen, based on your past experiences, prior to anything ever occurring.

If you heard a loud engine sound in the sky above you, before you even looked up, your mind would already predict that there was an airplane flying over you. Why? The answer is simple, in the past when you heard the same type of noise it was an airplane flying over you.

When you hear barking, you expect to see a dog. If you see someone smile at you, you expect that they are happy to see you. Unconsciously, we constantly, make these types of predictions. When you anticipate an event, your brain will prepare you for what it thinks is going to happen. If nothing has happened yet, you will mentally create the outcome and take actions to make this anticipated outcome a reality.

The mental process of creating expectations can work in your favor. If you increase the awareness of your thoughts and metacognition, the process of thinking about what you think about, you can begin to use your conscious mind to override your automatic thinking. This will allow you to change your expectations to match with what you want.

We all go through life creating expectations. The goal is not to eliminate expectations. Expectations are needed and help to reduce the stress and over-exertion of our brain. The goal should be, to align our expectations with what we want so we can take consistent actions to achieve what we desire.

What Now

Align your expectations with what you want:

1. **Become aware of your *E.T.A.*** – Get in touch with your **Emotions**, be conscious of your **Thoughts** and take **Actions** that move you toward your goal.
2. **Focus your mind.** – Consciously control what you say to yourself, the images you imagine and your actions.
3. **Explore your Expectations** – Periodically take time to just pause and reflect on what you are expecting. Imagine alternatives to what you have experienced in the past.

12

I Hear Voices

Be careful how you talk to yourself, because you are listening.

I remember, as a young boy, watching cartoons on Saturday morning and seeing certain characters who had a decision to make. An angel would show up on one shoulder and a devil would show up on the other. The angel would tell the character to do the right thing and share ideas about all the good they could bring to others and how. The devil on the other shoulder would say just the opposite. He would tell the character "you can never do it. That is for someone else to do. You don't have what it takes so just sit down and let someone else do it."

This is symbolic of what you go through on a daily basis. As you go about your journey you have these voices in your head talking to you.

What are you Thinking?

Which voice do you listen to? One voice may be encouraging you and sharing all the great things you are capable of achieving. While, at the same time, another voice is giving you all the reasons you are not able to achieve. You can imagine these voices as an angel and devil, a hero and a villain or an optimist and a pessimist. However you picture them, the voices you hear are your own.

Watching those cartoons as a kid played a role in programming my paradigm. It conditioned my mind to believe that when I had a decision to make there were options. What I didn't realize is that the voice which was louder was the one which usually represented how I unconsciously felt about myself.

As we talk about hearing voices, I want to be clear that this chapter is not speaking about auditory hallucinations. We are not speaking about mental conditions, such as schizophrenia, which can produce the sound of voices outside of the mind. This is about our inner speech (the silent expression of conscious thought to oneself in a coherent linguistic form.) Those things we say, internally, to ourselves throughout the day. Research shows that you speak about 4,000 words per minute to yourself on average.

Right now, as you read these words, you are more than likely talking to yourself. You may be talking about how you remember those cartoons or how you feel about this topic. We are in constant communication with ourselves. The question is "what are you saying?"

This inner speech has power and needs to be identified and harnessed. Your self-talk has the ability to either build you up or to tear you down. The things you say to yourself have a direct influence on your self-image and self-esteem. Albert Ellis, famed psychologist, once said, *"Self-esteem is the greatest sickness known to man or woman because it's conditional."* Most of the time, you are more than likely unaware of this internal conversation, because the majority of this self-talk is taking place in your unconscious mind.

There are times when your inner speech is a monolog and other times when it's a full-blown dialog. Either way, this is normal. There's nothing wrong with you. You are not the only one having a conversation with yourself.

A key to harnessing the power of this conversation is to consciously recognize when it is happening. Become aware and present, don't allow your unconscious mind to control the conversation. If you allow your unconscious mind to control what you are saying to yourself it will base everything on your past experiences, what you know right now, what others have said to you, and how you feel about what you have done in your life.

For some, this is a positive message. But, for most, it would be a message that revisits the negative situations they have experienced. It will constantly remind you of your "failures" and where you fell short of your goal. This process becomes the automatic default, if you don't interrupt your unconscious mind with positive comments. You must understand that we are programmed to focus on our short comings and to believe that what we want in life is beyond our control.

Think about what happens after you have done something people would consider embarrassing. What does your inner voice say to you? Does it say something like, "that was stupid?" What happens the next time you think about doing something similar? Your self-talk probably reminds you of the last time you did something like that, and it's usually not a nice conversation.

The things we say to ourselves can be very degrading and harsh. The words we use during our self-talk are words we usually won't consider saying to a loved one. Things like: *"I am such an idiot, I deserve to be alone, I am so fat, I am a failure or I'm not smart enough to get the promotion."* Besides these words being destructive, people don't realize the effects of saying them. Often times, your self-talk is just you telling yourself off.

Your inner speech is a combination of your conscious thoughts and your unconscious beliefs and biases. As you are having these self-talks you provide opinions and evaluations on what you're doing as you are doing it. They also allow a space for you to reflect on what has happened in the past.

Your mind will focus on the beliefs you have about yourself. If your unconscious mind can't see yourself being or achieving something, your brain will treat the thought as irrelevant. This is when you must take control of your thoughts, and this only happens when you heighten your awareness. Your brain must believe it's a waste of time and energy to think negative thoughts.

When you focus on the negative, what's not working, what you don't want, you are programming your reticular activating system (RAS.) This is the part of your brain that collects data from everything happening outside of you through your senses. You're programming your brain to find you more of the same. If you constantly allow the negative voice in your head to speak loudly to you, that data is being collected and your mind MUST find you more of those similar experiences in your world. But, the reverse is also true. If you allow the positive voice to speak loudly to you, your mind MUST find you more of the same. This is the natural function and process of the brain, no matter who you are. Your mind will only recognize those things around you which you are programmed to identify.

As a young child, you were probably told the story of "The Little Engine that Could," by Watty Piper. An early version of the story shares a tale of a little railroad engine that was built to pull a few train cars through the train yard.

One morning a long train of freight cars came in to the station. It begins to ask several of the large engines to take it over a large hill. One after another they refused, saying the train was too big for them to pull over the hill. These were engines designed and built to pull large trains. Out of desperation the freight train asked the little engine that was only built to pull a few cars to help. The little engine, without hesitation said, "I think I can." He got in front of the heavy train and began to pull the train toward the hill puffing faster and faster saying "I think I can, I think I can, I think I can."

As the small engine approached the top of the hill, it began to move slower. But, not giving up, it kept moving and saying, "I think I can, I think I can, I think I can." He finally made it to the top of the hill and went down the other side. Excited about what he had accomplished he began to puff, "I thought I could, I thought I could, I thought I could."

The odds were stacked against the little engine. By just looking at him, compared to the larger engines, you wouldn't have thought he would be the one to be able to get the freight over the hill. From the moment he was asked to pull the freight train, his self-talk was positive. He believed he could do it and he was conscious of what he said to himself.

When you are faced with a task, your success, is going to largely depend on how you feel about yourself. Not only how you feel about yourself, but also what you say to yourself. The little engine was confident in himself and said, over and over, "I think I can." This type of self-talk encourages you, it gives you the confidence to take the next step.

Do you think the little engine would have been able to accomplish the task if he said, "I'm too small," "I'm not strong enough" or "I'm not built for that?" No. If he had listened to the negative voice it would have stopped him dead in his tracks. And if you listen to the negative voice in your mind you will never fully live the life you were created and designed to live.

You will always hear voices, you are not trying to stop the voices. Be aware of them. Your goal is to control what voice you listen to and focus on. In turn this will help program your mind to find the things around you that will help you achieve your goals.

When you consciously hear yourself having negative self-talk, hit the mute button. Your mental mute button says, "I know you are there, but I am ignoring you." This is done through awareness and belief.

Understand, you have the right to believe or not to believe what the voices in your mind says. You are the only one with the power to accept a thought as truth. The differing thoughts you have are not a matter of good and bad, they are either truth or a lie. If you find yourself saying all the things you are not and cannot achieve, those are usually lies. You need to know the truth, and to understand that you must mute the lie.

When you find yourself in a position where you have a challenge, be aware of your inner speech. Hit the mute button on the negative voice. It doesn't matter if you don't have the skills needed to accomplish the goal in the beginning, just tell yourself, "I think I can." You may not have the necessary connections, but tell yourself, "I think I can." Even if you had bad experiences in your past, tell yourself, "I think I can." If you continue to move in the direction of your goal, you will one day be able to say to yourself, "I thought I could."

What Now

Why we have inner speech:
1. **Plan out your next step** – helps you talk through what you are planning.
2. **Reflect on the past** – Step through your experiences and learn what you can do different next time.
3. **Create alternative realities** - Inner speech has functions in imagination and this helps you see the future you want to have.
4. **To improve your performance** – athlete's and high achievers use it to motivate themselves.

13

That's Not Mine

Don't let the opinions of others consume you.

On your journey, there will be people that will suggest things that you should do in your life. Most of these offerings will be in good conscious, but may not directly correlate to your ultimate life goal. It seems that everyone always has ideas on what YOU should do with your life.

To prepare for these times, you should adopt the mindset of "That's Not Mine." What does that mean? This is a concept of you telling yourself "that's not mine" when you are given information that contradicts what you have desired for yourself. Everything that is said or suggested to you should not be ideas that you accept.

I remember being in grade school and someone had a handheld electronic football game that they were not supposed to have in class. The teacher saw it and asked who does that belong to, and someone said "Darius." My instant response was "that's not mine!" At that moment, and without much thought, I denied that the item belonged to me. In an act of self-preservation, I quickly defended myself.

Looking back over this event I can see how things could have gone differently, if I had allowed the other kid to say it was mine and I didn't respond. I would have been in trouble. Probably sent to the principal's office, and my parents may have been called. That would have brought on an entirely new issue once I got home. But because I didn't accept what the other kid said as truth, I removed myself from blame.

We all have, at some point in time, had a story similar to this story. A story where someone attempted to give you ownership of something that was not yours. It could have been a tangible object or a phrase that was said and you denied ownership.

My purpose in sharing this story is to give you some context as to when you may have used the phrase "that's not mine." The focus of this chapter is to put another spin on when you should say "that's not mine." It may sound childlike at times, but I believe it is an appropriate response depending on the situation.

I am not suggesting that you walk around telling people "that's not mine" all day. That would be weird. The message here is to awaken within your mind the awareness of what you are unconsciously accepting as truth and the effects.

There have been people who had opinions on what I should do with my life. They suggested colleges I should attend, careers I should pursue, woman I should date and everything else. Before I knew what I wanted out of life, I would listen to these suggestions. And on many occasions, I would take action based on what others told me I should do. However, what they believed I should be or do with my life never gave me a feeling of satisfaction or fulfilment.

Once I realized what I wanted to do with my life, I became stubborn. I stopped listening when people tried to convince me to do something that they felt I should do. What they wanted or suggested was not something that I believed would help me achieve my goals.

These were people who didn't know what I wanted out of life. They didn't have experience in what I wanted to accomplish. But they were well wishing, loving, friends, family members, and colleagues. They had good intentions, most of the time, but they were trying to get me to live my life through their experiences and beliefs.

After making the choice to take the advice of people like this and realizing that it was not getting me closer to my goal, I began to adopt the mindset of "that's not mine." I wouldn't say this to them. It was a statement I would make to myself. When they would try to push their beliefs on me, I would say to myself "that's not mine." If someone would share how they thought I should live my life, I would say, "that's not mine." If they didn't believe in my dream or believe I could accomplish something I would say to myself "that's not mine."

I began to live by the philosophy "**If someone tells you that you can't do something or you should do something different, smile, thank them and walk away like you never had the conversation.**"

I learned the hard way that there will be people who say things to you and about you that are not meant to help guide you to your desired destination in life. Now, when I feel that what someone is saying about me or to me is not a benefit to my goal, instead of getting upset or doubting myself, I say to myself "that's not mine."

You must understand that your brain can't distinguish between what you say and what someone else says. And if you don't put a disclaimer on statements made in ear shot of your brain, it will take it in as if you said it. "That's not mine" is a disclaimer to your brain to let it know that you are not the owner of that statement and you don't believe it or accept it.

Without hesitation, I will be the first to tell you that you need to take advice from others. You need to have mentors. I will also tell you that those you do take advice from need to have the knowledge, lifestyle and experiences that can guide you. Years ago, one of my mentors told me, "If you buy someone's opinion, you buy their lifestyle." You need to take a close look at those giving you advice, without judging them. Then decide if you had to change places with them would you be happy. Do they live a life that you want for yourself and family? Are they giving you advice that will help you achieve your goals?

Also take into consideration that many of the people in your life, who love you, are trying to protect you. They give advance under the notion of saving you from struggle. They may have gone through something similar to what you are about to embark on, and they just want to save you the heartache. Many believe their experience can provide an easier path for you.

There will be situations that you MUST go through to become who you are destined to be. In order to have the skillset, tools and experiences necessary to achieve your goal, you can't be saved or spared these challenges.

When I was in my early 20's I joined a Network Marketing company. I was excited! To me it appeared to be easy to sell some stuff and make some money. My thinking was "who wouldn't want to pay less for something they already use?" And who wouldn't want to make some extra money outside of what they were already doing? It just made sense to me.

But, to those close to me who didn't have the same experience thought it was a waste of my time. My parents, who I love dearly and I know love me, asked me why I was putting my time and money into this "thing." I had people come at me from everywhere saying it was a scam, I would not make any money, I am wasting my time, and it will never work because those "things" don't work. In my mind, I said to all of those people "that's not mine."

Their thoughts were not my thoughts. I was committed, and most people would have said "I drank the Kool-Aid." The most powerful part of all of this is that you would not be reading this book right now if I had not gone through the experiences I did in my Network Marketing career. That business is what turned me on to motivational speakers, reading books and listening to motivational audios in my car. I needed every one of the experiences I had during that journey.

It's like cutting a butterfly out of their cocoon to save them from the struggle of getting out on their own. Yes, you save them the struggle, but at same time you ruin their life because the struggle is what gives them the ability to fly. The butterfly would not be the beautiful graceful creature it is if it didn't struggle to get out of the cocoon.

If you have a dream, a goal, a desire to accomplish anything in life I strongly encourage you to adopt the mindset of "That's Not Mine." People will always share their thoughts, ideas and suggestions with you. And if they don't correlate to what your goal or dream is, say your disclaimer to yourself, "That's Not Mine" and keep pushing. There will be challenges and struggles. And just like the butterfly, they will build you up so you can fly. Become aware and be vigilant in protecting your thoughts.

— What Now —

1. **Be aware of everything that is being said and shown to you.** Either by TV, radio, social media, by phone or in person. If what you are taking in is not something that is guiding you toward your goal in life say to yourself **"That's Not Mine."**
2. **Understand that because someone loves you, that doesn't mean they know what you need.** There will be loved ones who share their thoughts with you, don't be so quick to accept what they share just because of your relationship.
3. **Embrace the struggle.** Even the beautiful butterfly had to struggle to become what it was destined to be. You too will have to struggle at some point. Stay focused on your goal. Sometimes you won't know the reason for the struggle until you get through it.

14

They're Giving Away Average

Greatness never goes on sale.

Few people will admit to chasing average. If you take a serious look at society, you will see that society doesn't celebrate or compensate average well. If you are considered to be average you are not being bombarded with invites to big events or asked to share your story. The paparazzi is not outside your front door or following you around. They are not saying things like "hey there is Joe Average, get his picture, let's talk to him."

I believe that every one of us has been put here for a reason. And that reason is different for everyone. But, it boggles my mind when I think about this and I see the basic routine of most people's lives look exactly the same.

If you take the sum of the whole and divide it by the number that makes up the whole you will get the average. If the majority is just skating by, doing just enough to make it and not moving toward the reason they are here, then most people fall in the median. What does that mean? That means most people are average.

To be average doesn't take much effort. But if you ask the question: Do you believe you are average? Most people will answer by saying, no. They will argue that they are different from everyone else. But, when you move all the weeds out of the way and look at what they actually do (their actions and activities) and listen to what they say, it will probably be the "norm" that you get from the masses.

Average pushes everybody in the same direction, at the same pace, to go to the same place. When I think of "average" I create an image of herding cattle. When they herd cattle, they gather all the cows and march them in the same direction and usually want them to keep the same pace, so they all stay together. The final destination the majority of the time is the slaughter house.

It is unfortunate, but we are surrounded by people with this "herd mentality." They move with their head down looking at the ground (or their smart phone), not looking at where they are going, just blindly following the person in front of them, with no goals to focus on. The only thing missing is the mooing.

If you step back and look at rush hour traffic, it closely resembles herds of cattle. Everyone going in the same direction, at about the same pace, going to similar destinations. It may not be directly to the slaughter house, but it's like the living dead how they are living their life.

What is average? In the case of human beings and their achievements, average is a word used to compartmentalize the masses. After selling the population on the idea of comparing themselves to each other, it was easy to start grouping people together. Ironically, those that made up the "average" group outnumbered everyone else.

It seems most people became happy to be average. Society made it easy for you to become a part of the group. They are actually giving away average. If you do just enough, compare your life with others who are average, and don't step out of the box you were put in, you can be average.

With the masses being average, it allowed for a small group to become "high achievers" and the opportunity to stand out. The high achievers went above and beyond. This is the group that the average people look up to. The majority of the average group idolizes the high achievers. They dream of one day being successful and joining the "high achievers." The magic of the high achievers' group is that it doesn't take that much more than what most in the average group do to join.

Just as there is a small portion of the population that have done better than those who are average, there is also a small group that have not done as well. This group of "low performers" enable those that are average to feel good about themselves. If someone is average they can compare themselves to someone who is a low performer and say, "at least we are doing better than them."

The Bell curve that was created to graphically depict these groups always shows the masses in the middle. This model is used to compare people in many different categories. It can be used to compare weight, height, age, income, number of children and the like. But at the end of the day, this can box people in. This can put you in a place that has you believe that is all that you can achieve.

There are many who would say they were above average. They are doing well for themselves, comparatively. They are like the big fish in a small pond. Most fish that are kept in a tank will only grow as big as the tank allows. If the fish is to continue to grow to its fullest potential, it must be moved to a bigger tank.

Understand that you were designed to grow. If you become complacent and stop growing, that is the moment you begin dying. Many that outgrow their tank become afraid to become the small fish in the ocean. They don't want to step up to the next level because it may expose their short comings. This fear shows that most people are more afraid of not being enough to compete with those with more skills, talent and ability than learning something new and being challenged.

There's nothing inspiring about being average! Since birth we have been taught to compare ourselves with others. The biggest issue with this is that we are not comparing ourselves with the best of the best, we are comparing and being compared to those in the middle of the pack. The conformity of comparing yourself to someone else, creates the mindset of "I have to be like them."

They are giving away average! It is a choice to accept it. You need to develop the mindset that you are "allergic to average." Start coughing, sneezing, and break out in hives when you think that what you are doing is average. Jump out of the box. You were created to be unique, an original.

You can only be average if you accept that you are like the masses. Average is a mindset. There will be many, that are average, that will attempt to change your thoughts. They will try to convince you that it is alright to be average. Once you believe that you are not average, no one will be able to tell you otherwise.

This can be a struggle. I know this to be true for myself. There are many times when I look at what I am doing and I know that I can do more and do better. I, just like you, have been conditioned my entire life to be similar to everyone else. To stay out of the average column I consciously remind myself that I am different. Different is amazing! And different will keep you out of being average.

It's a slippery slope to average. The choice is yours and yours alone. You are the only one that can truly determine what you are going to be.

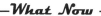

What Now

4 Steps to avoid being Average.

1. **Become Allergic to Average** –This is a mindset. How can you program your mind to feel uncomfortable when you are not doing your best? You are looking to create a visceral reaction. To create this mindset, you need to be conscious and you must turn off autopilot. If you are honest, and realize you are not doing your best work, attach the feeling of discomfort to the thought of you not doing your best. This will get your attention so you can step up a level.

2. **Ease is the enemy** – Our brain is wired for easy. It doesn't take hard work to be average. Being true to yourself may take hard work. You may have to retrain your brain. There are certain things you must go through. The butterfly will not fly if you cut it out of the cocoon. You have to create the mindset that you will not always avoid difficulty.
3. **Demand higher performance from yourself.** There's nothing inspiring about being average when you are capable of being remarkable. Mediocrity is the road most traveled. You have a choice, you can decide that you are going to follow the pack or veer off and pave the way. When you are faced with a choice, think about your response and base a decision on if it will lead to mediocrity or you performing at a higher level.
4. **Accept encouragement rather than coddling.** Coddling accepts poor performance. This is what we look for when we want to feel good. This doesn't inspire you to step up and do better. Encouragement says you can reach higher and pushes you to step out of your comfort zone. Starting today, seek feedback from someone that will push you to do better. Don't look for someone who will just tell you what you want to hear. Ask this question to those you seek feedback from: What could I have done better? You need to be pushed, not stroked.

15

Garbage In, Garbage Stays

What you put in your head is going to create your life.

Let me ask you: What are you feeding your mind?

Too often we don't pay attention to what we are putting into our mind. In this day and time of information overload we must be cognizant of what information we take in. Your mind is like a sponge, it will absorb whatever you feed it. You have been programmed to believe that what you put in, comes out. This philosophy is not accurate when you are investing in your self-development.

Several years ago, in a private training session with the legendary, world-renowned inspirational speaker and author, Mr. Les Brown, we were talking about the type of information we consume on a daily basis. The conversation was open and a few people shared what they were reading or listening to at the time. Mr. Brown talked about the information that he would read and listen to when he was first getting started in the speaking business. This was insightful for me. I always wondered what great and accomplished people read or listen to when the lights and cameras are turned off.

His face lit up when he began to reminisce about the early days of his illustrious speaking career. I remember thinking to myself: "Wow, I want to look back one day and feel as elated about my start as a speaker, regardless of the struggles and hard times." As the conversation went on and people were sharing, laughing and unknowingly growing, Mr. Brown stood up, and in his deep attention demanding voice said: "Garbage in…" And everyone yelled "Garbage out." To everyone's surprise he blurted out a huge "NO!" He replied, "Garbage Stays!"

That's right, **Garbage In…Garbage Stays!**

This was a pivotal moment in my mental growth. From that point on I began to evaluate what I allowed into my head. I set a goal to only consume content which added value to my life. Prior to that, I lived my life and made decisions based on how my paradigm was programmed as a child.

You begin with a clean slate at birth. Everything is new and you attempt to absorb it all. As an infant you are trying to figure out who you are, what you are and how you fit in. Unfortunately, during this stage, you don't have much control over what you are exposed to.

By ages 5 to 7, the basis of your paradigm has been programmed. You already have your basic beliefs about yourself and the world around you. This programming was done by those raising you. During this time, you are also creating habits. The person you are today has a lot to do with this programming. What you must understand is that, you were not in control of how you were being programmed.

Most adults are still living their lives based on how they were programmed as children. If you asked them, they probably don't know why they believe what they believe. They have never challenged what they were taught. Regardless, if it was garbage or great information, they will defend it because it is what they believe.

Every day you continue to program your paradigm. This is done by consuming information. This information can be taken in by what you read, listen to, watch on TV, conversations you have with others and what you say to yourself. If what you are allowing into your mind is garbage, it will stay and you will begin to make decisions based on that information.

Why is this important to understand? Here's why, if you are consistently feeding your mind negative thoughts, images and ideas (what I consider garbage) you program the unconscious part of your mind. When you decide you want to pursue your dreams the unconscious mind will pull up those negative thoughts and images and remind you of the things you believe. Especially, if it is what you believe about yourself. If those thoughts don't correlate to your new journey you will have an internal battle going on within your mind.

For many, very few positive seeds have been planted in the garden of their mind. So, when they decide to do something different they are reminded that they are not good enough, they are not smart enough or they are not special. All the thoughts they had, come back up at the time when they are looking for encouragement to move forward in their journey.

What's interesting to me is that instead of fighting and flushing those thoughts out, most people agree with them and let them take over, like weeds. Hence, the feeling of being stuck. Your mind is a powerful tool, and so it is a challenge to get it to go against what it knows and believes.

If you take a gallon of pure water, and put one drop of contaminated water into it, you will now have a gallon of contaminated water. Just like the water, it doesn't take much to contaminate your mind.

If you wanted to have a gallon of pure water again what would you have to do? How do you get back to pure water? You don't have a filter, you can't just scoop out the contaminated water. Once it is mixed in, that's it, it's in there.

To have a gallon of pure water again, you will have to pour out all the water and clean out the container. Or, you will have to pour fresh water into the container and let it over flow until it clears out all the contaminated water. This process may take a while and much more than a gallon of water will be needed to clear out the contaminated water.

What does this mean in terms of your thoughts and your mind? If you put garbage in your mind and you want to begin to clear it out, you can't take off the top of your head and dump out what's in there. That's not possible. What you must do is start to flush out the negative with positive. To get to zero (or close to it) you will need to have more positive thoughts than negative thoughts. You may need to

O.D. on positive information, quotes, and positive self-talk to get yourself on neutral ground.

Recently my wife and I have been very conscious about our health. As we get older we usually become aware of the things that we may have done to our bodies over the years. There comes a time, when you get up in the morning and it takes a minute to get out of the bed. You don't just jump up and your feet hit the floor and you are ready to tackle the day. You may wake up and you hear things cracking or you're stiff and need a minute just to kind of stretch things out.

I went to the doctor not long ago because my body was not reacting the way it used to when I was younger. A reason for this was due to what I had been feeding my body. I didn't think those hamburgers I ate over the years would have much of an effect on me, or those sodas would cause any problems. The reality was that eating those types of foods had started to have an effect and my body was rejecting and fighting what was left behind.

Your mind operates the same way. Garbage in…garbage stays. When you decide to pursue your dreams, you will be reminded of the garbage you put in. At the time, when you are feeding your mind you don't pay much attention. When you don't have an instant response, you are tricked into believing that it has no effect.

If garbage in…garbage out was a true statement you wouldn't have after effects of negative thoughts. Once you had a negative thought it would just leave your mind totally. You would be able to flip a mental switch and focus on what you wanted to achieve without doubt. The lack of truth of this statement is proven when you have thoughts of fear, lack of belief and feeling unworthy.

You teach your unconscious mind everything it knows. Your actions, emotions and feelings are not random. They are automatically triggered when you have an experience, by the thoughts you have stored in your unconscious mind. If you are not aware of the negative thoughts that your conscious mind is telling your unconscious mind, you are not in control of what you are thinking. This has a major effect on every decision you make, every desire you have and every goal you want to achieve.

Here is something else you need to be aware of, your unconscious mind does not have the ability to distinguish between a positive thought and a negative thought. It will simply take the thought that is destructive and make it real, just as it will with a constructive thought. Another layer of danger to being unaware of your thoughts is that this also aids you in developing your self-image.

Your mind will choose to accept or reject certain thoughts that you create or someone else tells you, based on if it believes it is useful to your self-image. If you have a negative picture of yourself, negative thoughts will be accepted and reinforce your beliefs. These thoughts will stay in your unconscious mind for as long as you allow them to.

If you have accepted as your reality that you are fat, based on what someone else may have said to you years ago, that thought remains in your unconscious. It will be triggered any time you are in a situation that requires you to show your body. If you are thinking about the summer or going to the beach and putting on a bathing suit, you will feel anxious and maybe even depressed. Attempts at losing weight will always fail, if you haven't challenged the thoughts you have about yourself. If you think "I want to lose weight, but I don't think I will be able to do it," you will never lose weight. You will always "want to lose weight," but you will never believe "you will be able to."

If you are ready to challenge your garbage thoughts and clear them out of your mind, you must recognize that you are having them. Ignoring the thoughts or acting like they are not there does not stop them from being accepted by your unconscious. A paradigm shift is needed. You need a modification in the thoughts you have and an understanding of how to flush out the thoughts you don't want. The goal of this process is to have your conscious and unconscious thoughts in sync with one another. Acknowledge when you have a thought. Question that thought to see if it supports what you want and if it doesn't replace it with one that does.

Feeding your mind garbage for years will produce unwanted outcomes and actions. These thoughts do not go in one ear and out the other. Making the commitment to flushing out the negative is imperative to a success filled life. Creating the habit of focusing on healthy, positive thoughts starts with making the decision that it is worth fighting for your dreams.

What Now

5 Actions to reduce accepting garbage thoughts:

1. **Pay attention** – Be aware of the thoughts you are having and what you are letting into your mind. If you understand that what goes in and is not challenged stays, you are better equipped to dismiss negative thoughts.
2. **Only consume content that adds value** – It is vital that you monitor what you listen to, watch, read and talk about. Consume content that is in line with your goals.
3. **Reframe your thoughts** – Put a positive spin on any negative thought that comes into your mind. A simple change in words you use can have a huge impact on the outcome of your decisions. Instead of saying "I don't believe I can do it," say "I will find a creative way to do it." What you desire to do needs to be backed up and supported with positive and supportive thoughts.
4. **Question the thoughts you have** – Ask yourself a few questions about your thoughts like, "Is this true?" "Says who?" "Do I like this thought?" "Do I want to keep this thought or dismiss it?" Many times, we base our beliefs and actions on assumptions. We make decisions about things that have not happened and probably won't happen the way we think.
5. **Change your physical state** – Your posture makes a difference in your thinking. If you are slouching and frowning you will, more than likely, be in a negative thought pattern. If you sit up, smile and breathe deeply you can bring in more positive thoughts and feelings.

16
Did You Want That?

Are you going after what you want in life, or what you think you can achieve? There is a difference.

If you are only doing enough to get what you think you can have, you will never get what you actually want. This thinking and mindset will not inspire you to go beyond your limited beliefs.

There are many factors and reasons why people don't go after what they really want in life. We all, every single one of us, have been given a dream or vision of what our life can be at some point in time. We hear stories all the time of people who take that vision and run with it and sometimes they change cultures, lives and even the world. NEWS FLASH: Those that have taken this path are not free from discouragement or opposition or even obstacles in their path. What makes them push through these barriers is a belief that they can do it. It's really that simple. They believe!

We will only pursue that in which we believe we can accomplish. Here we have personal enemy number 1: lack of self-belief.

When people think about what they want and they can't see HOW they can make it happen they pull the vision back. They literally scale down the goal. Here is the issue with this thinking; It is impossible to figure out the "How", before you know the what. You can't say "this is how I'm going to do such and such", if you don't know what such and such is.

Think about what it is that you REALLY want to do. This is your vision not mine or anyone else's. When you are thinking about what you want, remember that your vision and dream are invisible to everyone else. No one was in your head when God gave you the vision. When you think about what you want and think back to when you had this vision for the first time, the "HOW" was probably not a part of the "What." You were not given the vision of what your purpose is and how to accomplish it at the same time.

I believe that you would not have been given the vision or dream to do something if you didn't have the capacity to fulfil it. Dr. Martin Luther King, Jr once said "Take the first step in faith. You don't have to see the whole staircase, just take the first step." At the moment of inception of the dream, you may not have all of the knowledge or know-how on how to bring that dream to fruition. This does not mean that it is not destine for you to have. What it does tell you is that you have work to do, things to learn and failures to complete. Yes FAILURES. This is how we learn, trial and error. Don't dodge failure, embrace it, it is part of the process.

Along your journey you will develop the skills, wills and insight on how to achieve your goal. You may need to go back to school. You may need to sign up for seminars and online training courses. *You definitely need to read, and re-read, this book.* You will have to learn more than you know right now. What you know right now has gotten you to where you are!

If you begin to pay attention to what is being presented on your journey, there will be opportunities shown to you that will allow you to gain the knowledge, skills and insights needed to achieve your dream. The "HOW" will show up out of your commitment to the "What."

This chapter is about you taking a conscious look at what you are working and fighting for. Most people are going after what they think they can achieve, instead of going after what they really want.

I mentioned a little earlier that there are many factors why people don't go after what they really want. One of the biggest factors is they simply don't BELIEVE.

Is lack of believe holding you back? Or do you believe you can accomplish great things? Most people don't believe they have what it takes to accomplish the dream and vision they were given. This is proven every day. They won't do what is necessary to move in the direction of their goal. They won't find a mentor or take that class or go to that seminar because they don't believe it will help them.

The HOW doesn't matter if you don't believe. Instead of saying they don't believe most will say "they are being realistic." Your reality is based on your perception. Their temporary situation doesn't provide the light at the end of the tunnel, so they turn their back on their true calling.

Belief is a factor that can stop people from going after what they truly want. Or should I say, "Lack of Belief."

Here's another factor that prevents people from going after their goals: FEAR! Fear makes people react, instead of respond. When we are afraid our amygdala takes over and we go into fight or flight mode. We take action based on past experiences that we have had. We usually don't pause and think about what outcome we want and how our response will help determine that outcome. We just freeze, run in the opposite direction or tell ourself it can't be true.

So, if you have an opportunity come your way and the benefits are amazing and looks like you can't lose, most people will say "it must be too good to be true." This is a fear-based statement. And it is usually based on what someone else has experienced and shared with you at some point.

There are many things that people are afraid of. From how they will look to others, to not succeeding, to thinking they will lose what they have and so on. Because of these fears they don't do anything. This leads down the path of just accepting what has been given and never focusing on what they really want out of life. They begin to tell themselves "I'm good." Fear often causes us to lie to ourselves.

Let's talk about one more factor that stops people from going after their goal. **Appearance**. When you think about the word appearance, what comes to mind? Most would say how you look. I would like to ask a follow up question.

How you look to whom? It is usually how you look to other people.

This is a huge factor in people not going after what they want with all they have. They are worried about their appearance. How are they going to look to others? What is "everyone" going to say about me if I do this?

People are constantly making decisions based on what they think others will say or think of them. If this is you, let me ease your mind. Nobody is paying that much attention to your life! And if you don't share everything that is going on with you on Social Media, no one will know. So many people put so much time, energy and effort into making sure people see them a certain way that they forget about their vision and goal.

When horses are about to race, the jockey and trainer prepare the animal. One of the things they make sure they do is put blinders on the horse. If you ever watched a horse race you will see that every horse on the track has on blinders. What is the purpose of this? Does it make them run faster? Does it make them aerodynamic? The real reason that the horses wear blinders is so that they don't look at the other horses during the race. If they start to focus on another horse they will misstep and fall or begin to slow up.

If you are fighting to achieve a goal or fulfill your vision, you need to put on your mental blinders. When you start to look and listen to what other people say, you will misstep or begin to slow up.

Here's what I know for sure! When people share their thoughts and suggestions about what you are doing with you, it is based on their beliefs and experiences. If you accept them, you are saying you believe what they believe. Here is how this looks and sounds: 'Darius, I don't think you would be a good author." I, in turn, decide not to write this book. The true result of this is not just me not stepping up and writing the book, but me unconsciously saying "I believe you, I would not be a good author."

The other part that we rarely talk about is what happens next. The next part of this transaction is JUSTIFICATION. People in this situation now justify why they didn't do what they said they originally wanted to do. They say things like "I don't have time" or "This will take me away from my family" or "I will have to work long hours." Sound familiar?

There will be countless excuses as to why they didn't do something. They will say everything besides the true reason. Which is "I believed what someone else believed about me." This only leads to someone not going after what they truly envisioned for their life.

So, when you look at where you are in your life, ask yourself "Did I want that?" Did you want what you have? Is what you have and where you are what you envisioned for your life? If not, you may need to take a look at why you made certain decisions and see if you lacked self-belief, had fear, or worried about your appearance to others. These are only a few factors in why people settle for what they have instead of fighting for what they want.

There will always be forces against what you are attempting to do. This doesn't mean you have to settle. It means you must get stronger. Move forward knowing that you MUST believe in yourself. You will face fear, and people will attempt to distract you from your goal. If you know this going in, it will prepare you to deal with it when it happens.

Accomplishing your goal and dream will not be easy, but once you achieve it I believe you will think it was worth it. Eleanor Roosevelt was quoted as saying **"You must do the thing you think you cannot do."** YOU MUST!

What Now

---

1. **Give yourself permission to think bigger** - "It doesn't take any more effort to dream a big dream than it does to dream a small dream." Gen. Wesley Clark said. If you have an idea of what you want or want to do with your life, take a second and increase the dream. If you say you want to get a BS degree, why not step it up and work to get a Master's degree. Whatever it is you want, think of ways you can stretch yourself to your true potential.
2. **If you're scared, say you're scared** – There is nothing wrong with being afraid, but there is everything wrong with allowing it to stop you from achieving your dream. Fear is just an emotion that we created to protect us from harm. Once you realize that you are not in harm's way push forward toward your goal. Most people fear things that never happen.
3. **Put Your blinders on** – Race horses wear blinders for a reason. They want to limit the distractions as they run toward their goal. This is the same reason you need to wear your mental blinders when you are around people who don't see your vision. Don't be distracted by outside negative influences.

17

Start First, Learn During

Anything that you want to accomplish, you first must start.

I know, this sounds so elementary. You may be saying "Darius why are you talking about stuff we already know." My answer, "Most people don't act like they know." There is no head start or short cuts to your dreams. You will never reach the goal line standing still. Too often people are looking to see what the end will be before they make the commitment of that first step.

Their thinking is "If you can guarantee me that the outcome will be what I want, I will do it." The only guarantee any of us have is that if you are living and breathing right now, one day (hopefully no time soon) you will die. That is the only guarantee. Too often people are looking for the guarantee (the end result) before they commit.

So, let me ask you: Have you started? Have you taken the first step towards your goal, your dream? Before you can accomplish anything, I mean anything, you must start first. Starting doesn't mean knowing everything you need to do. Starting doesn't mean you have step-by-step actions for the entire process mapped out. There will be things you will figure out along the way.

You should have a plan for how you will start, what will be the first few actions you will need to take. That is fine and even advised. I suggest that you have some sort of plan. Just understand as you go and grow, there will be things that you could not anticipate before you started.

One issue with starting is that it can be extremely scary to most. Here is my remedy for fear, "If you're scared, say you're scared." It is alright to be scared. This is where you have to put your big boy or big girl pants on and feel the fear, respect the fear, acknowledge the fear and tell the fear that I am going to do it anyway.

This fear is usually based on ignorance. Ignorance is nothing more than "the lack of knowledge or knowing." Ignorance can be rectified. Many times, when we start something new we are ignorant to some of the details. Ignorant to the steps, the process, the feelings we will have and the outcome. Something that will help you with this is experience. Experience gives us the knowledge we will need to overcome most of our fears.

Over 20 years ago I started a career as a software trainer. I was pumped and excited about my new career. I was what I have heard people call "ignorance on fire." I was so ready, but I had absolutely no clue how my first class was going to go. I was young, had never taught a computer class and the

Start First, Learn During

class was comprised of people much older than me and I was quietly terrified. Just thinking about standing in front of that room had me shook.

On the day of my first class I stood in the back of the room while the person hosting the training event introduced me. At that moment I gave myself permission to be scared and nervous. Sometimes the only permission you need is your own. Also, I realized that I could never say I taught my first class if I didn't start and teach my first class.

I could have easily made excuses. It would not had been hard for me to act like I was sick or say I forgot something or rescheduled the class. But, if I would have walked out and not started I would have still been in the same situation, I would not have been able to say, "I taught my first class."

I had been studying and practicing for this moment for weeks. But as I was slowly walking to the front of the room I had all kinds of conversations going on in my head. I thought about the hours I put in getting ready, I thought about "what if they don't think I can teach them anything because they are older than me", I thought about "what if I mess up and say the wrong thing", "what if the computers don't work" (even though I checked them all before the class came in.) I also thought about the class laughing, learning and having a good time. I thought about how I would feel if I got rave reviews after class was over. This seemed like the longest walk ever. My mind was racing and my heart was thumping.

There were so many things that I knew I had to learn but I would have never learned them if I didn't start. What I learned DURING this process and my first class are intangibles that I could not have learned reading a book or watching a video. This experience taught me that there will be things that you can only learn during your journey. You can't learn how to swim by reading a book.

I had to **START FIRST, THEN LEARN**.

I will tell you that my first class went pretty well. I didn't mess up too bad. The participants in the training class gave me some great compliments and feedback on their experience. It led me to begin to love speaking and helping people achieve their goals.

Because of this experience I didn't have the same fears going into my next class. But if I had not started and taught that first class I would have still had those same fears.

What is it that you know you should be doing, but because of fear or ignorance, you have not started? On this journey called life you have ideas and your intuition tells you that you should be doing certain things. But, because we don't think we know enough or at that moment have what it takes, we never start.

As you think about this I want you to know that when you start something, that doesn't mean you are not prepared. You need to prepare to start. If you are going to go jogging you must first put on your work out gear, put on and lace up your running shoes and stretch.

When I was scheduled to teach my first class, I prepared for weeks for that event. I studied the material I was teaching, how to present it and how to answer questions.

There will be a prep process for the journey you are going to start. The specific task necessary will vary based on what it is that you are looking to accomplish. Figuring out what those are is part of the preparation process.

You may not know what the 2nd, 3rd and 4th steps are before you start. Take comfort in knowing that if you don't, it's alright. And even if you do, things may not go as you have planned.

As I am writing these words, my oldest daughter, in her sophomore year of college. Before she went to freshman orientation, moved into her dorm room and took her first class, do you think she knew everything that she needed to know to earn her college degree? No. Of course not. My wife and I didn't expect for her to know all of that. As a matter of fact, she didn't even know her way around campus that well.

Our expectation for her was to learn as she goes. Now that she has finished her first year, she knows a lot more about what it will take and what she needs to do, but she still doesn't know everything. Because of her experiences over the past year she has gained knowledge that now assist her in making decisions that will impact the next steps in her journey.

Far too many people never start because they feel they don't know "EVERYTHING" they need to know. This is a mindset trap that holds people back from ever having the success they desire. The conversations that we have with ourselves every day provide the foundation for what we believe. If you have been telling yourself that there is more that you need to know before you start, you won't start until you know that information. The issue here is, that may be information that will not be available until you reach a few milestones in your journey first. This puts you in a no-win situation.

Many brilliant ideas have never come to fruition because someone didn't start. I believe the number one reason most people never start is because their brain is proving them right. You say you can't do it, and your brain goes to work to prove that you are right, you can't do it. If you have a fear of what will happen, that will activate your amygdala. The amygdala is designed to protect you from danger or harm, so it will begin your fight, flight or freeze response. In this state of mind, nothing will get done because you become frozen in time.

Your mind will constantly try to keep you safe. It will attempt to hold you back from trying anything new. If you seek to do something you have never done before this will create uncertainty, and your brain seeks certainty. Being aware of this process of the brain gives you an advantage, because now you are in control. When you feel yourself starting to freeze or run from your goal, you can tell yourself that there is no danger. You can reinforce that you are safe and calm your brain so you can make the decisions necessary to start your journey.

The answers will come, the know-how will come, and the clarity will come, during the journey. So, just get started.

What Now

Five proactive steps you can take to get started.

1. **Just jump** – Don't dip your toe in the pool to see if the water is cold, just jump. Go all in and be assured

that you will learn what to do DURING your journey.
2. **Control your tongue and thoughts** – manage your negative self-talk. Be aware of what you are saying to yourself.
3. **Say it with your chest** – Show confidence. Believe in your abilities.
4. **Seek guidance and advice** – Get a mentor. Find someone who has done what it is that you are looking to do and ask for help/feedback. Step out, don't hide. You can't take this journey by yourself.
5. **Invest in yourself** – There are skills you will need to learn and develop. Make the time and money investment necessary to learn the skills you need.

18
Everything You Do Matters

"Act as if what you do makes a difference because it does." William James

Everything you do matters. Even the "little things." There are so many people that walk around thinking that only the "big" decisions they make are the ones that have an impact. This thinking lends credence to not paying attention to every thought, action, and deed.

In 1963 a gentleman by the name of Edward Lorenz wrote a doctoral thesis called "The Butterfly Effect." You may be familiar with his work or the premise behind his thesis. The theory of The Butterfly Effect stated that a butterfly could flap its wings on one side of the world and set molecules of air in motion that set other molecules of air in motion, causing a chain reaction and on the other side of the world create a hurricane or some other weather event.

When Lorenz first presented this idea, he was laughed at. (Side note: If people think you are crazy that doesn't mean they are right.) But, the idea hung around for years, people wrote books about it and created a movie based on the theory. Physics professors proved that The Butterfly Effect was correct. They found that it was accurate and viable and it worked every time.

Scientists discovered that this worked not just with butterflies but with any moving object, including people. It has since been made a law in the scientific world. The Butterfly Effect is now known as **The Law of Sensitive Dependence upon Initial Conditions**.

I view the idea of "everything you do matters" the same as I do The Butterfly Effect. It is a universal law, and universal laws always work. Here is what is important, this law works whether you know it or not. It works regardless of your knowledge of its existence. Much like the law of gravitation. Before Sir Isaac Newton verbalized and developed the science behind the law of gravity, there was still gravity. People were not just floating around the earth. This law was in effect and working prior to a name for it. Just because you don't understand the law of gravity doesn't mean that if you stumble off a cliff you won't fall to your death.

I need you to understand that there is a universal law that is the foundation of "Everything You Do Matters." Too often we take for granted small things that we do on a daily basis. We move through our lives as if what we did yesterday has no effect on today. This is not true.

The idea of the butterfly flapping its wings didn't say that the hurricane on the other side of the world would happen as soon as the butterfly started flapping. What it implies is that the flapping of the wings would affect one thing that then would affect something else that would then affect something else and eventually cause a hurricane.

So, what you may be doing today; in a week, a month, a year, or even decades can affect your life and the lives of others.

In the early 1940's a woman found herself at home alone while her husband was off serving in the military. She connected with another man and this relationship resulted in her becoming pregnant with twins. In February of 1945 she went into labor. She was embarrassed and ashamed of what she had done, so she went into an abandoned building with a mid-wife and had twin boys on the linoleum floor. She loved her babies and wanted the best for them but knew she couldn't provide it to them. She told the mid-wife to give her boys to someone who would love and take care of them. The mid-wife agreed. She found a woman who couldn't have children but wanted them. This lady took in the twins raised them the best she could. She didn't have much money and worked as a maid to provide for her family. One day she took one of the boys with her to a house she was cleaning. It was a huge house and the little boy said, "Momma, one day I am going to buy you a house just like this." She said "okay."

That little boy had a tough time in school but met a man, a teacher at the time, who took him in and mentored him. He graduated from school and fell in love with the disc jockeys on the radio. He begged a radio station owner to hire him and after several uninvited visits he was hired as an errand boy. He studied the DJ's and practiced what he would say if he ever got a chance to be on the air.

That day came and he was ready. He ended up becoming a DJ after that day. Later, he was told by his mentor that he was more than a DJ. He didn't believe that about himself but he believed in his mentor. Eventually this man became a public speaker, he wrote books and brought his mother that house.

After many years in the speaking field he meets a gentleman by the name of Barry. Barry was a top leader in a business that I was introduced to many years ago. Barry owned a training center in Chicago and had an event and invited this speaker to come and speak. I heard about the event and went to Chicago to meet this man. I had been introduced to his work years before and loved what he did. In Chicago, I meet this man and he told me he was having an event in Annapolis, Md. This was not far from where I lived. I signed up for it and took my wife. This man became a mentor of mine and changed my life. My desire to become a speaker went through the roof after meeting and working with him.

This man's name is Les Brown. What if his biological mother would have had an abortion? What if his adopted mother would have never taken him to work with her that day? What if he would have never met Barry? What if I had never joined that business and met Barry?

All the decisions and actions in this story mattered. Even at the time no one was aware of what would result from them. If it didn't work out the way it did, I may not have written this book or became a speaker. Then you would not be reading these pages right now. And your life may not be changed because of it. This is The Butterfly Effect. Everything you do or don't do matters forever.

There are multiple things happening at this exact moment that have the power to change the course of your life. The actions that you take or don't take are going to determine which direction you will go.

Some people will call it fate. What is for you, is for you. Everything that has happened was supposed to happen, and happen the way it did happen. And to a certain point I agree. But if you are just sitting at home waiting for something to drop in your lap, you're going to be sitting for a long time.

You may be reading these words thinking to yourself that your life has had no major significance. But, a simple smile at a passing stranger may have stopped them from committing suicide or gave them the confidence they needed to go to that job interview. In this time of Likes, Comments and Shares on Social Media, we have developed a false sense of significance. The truth is, it doesn't matter who clicks the like button. Who you become, the lives you may impact and how you leave your mark on the world may happen without much engagement. That doesn't mean that it is not happening. I know that the biological mother of Les Brown was not thinking about how her decision to give up her twin boys was going to positively impact my life decades later.

This law doesn't just pertain to what you put out into the world. It also impacts what happens within you. If you have a goal in life and you are focused on achieving this goal, what you do matters.

What you listen to matters, what you read matters, who you associate with matters. These things are critical to you becoming who you are destined to be. If you are feeding your mind with positive energy and information, your actions will be positive. If you are feeding your mind negative, your actions will be negative.

Be aware of what you are letting into your mind. It is easy to get distracted and let your guard down and let in negative energy. You must keep in mind that your brain doesn't know if you said something or if it came from someone else.

The content that you consume from social media is not exempt. So, if you spend your time watching videos, reading post, and having conversations about negative events, that is being stored in your mind. Garbage in, garbage stays! This will always have an effect on your thinking and the decisions you make.

Oprah Winfrey has a rule. Whenever she travels she has a rule for whoever is driving the car that picks her up. The rule is that when she gets in the car the radio is turned off. The reason that she has this rule is because she is focused on protecting her mind.

Everything matters so protect what you let in. Be aware of what you put out. The decisions you make or don't make, the actions you take or don't take all have an impact. Go about your life with the consciousness of knowing what you are doing does matter.

The Law of Sensitive Dependence upon Initial Conditions implies that what you do will not only affect your life but the lives of others. When people are not open to the reality that what they do has a ripple effect, they become selfish. And when you have been given a dream and you don't go after it and fulfill that dream, you hold back that person you were designed to help achieve their dream.

The late rapper and actor, Tupac Shukar, said in an interview "I may not change the world, but I will spark the brain of the person who will." You may be the brain that he spoke about, or you may be one of the ones who will spark the brain of the person who will change the world.

What Now

Everything you do matters so:

1. Be Kind.
2. Be Thoughtful.
3. Be Aware.
4. Consume content that adds value.
5. Stay in a positive vibration.
6. Smile.
7. Protect your mind.
8. Know you make a difference.
9. Pay attention.
10. Be open.
11. Have a growth mindset.
12. Think clearly, deliberately and intentionally.

19

Constant Contradiction

You should always be evolving. Part of this evolution should be you thinking differently.

When you change how you think you change how you see things. This change usually brings contradiction to what you may have once thought. Changing how you think and contradicting what you thought in the past is not always a bad thing.

When you run into an old classmate, friend or family member you haven't seen you in years, they should not be reuniting with the same person mentally. This is part of the reason why we grow apart from people. We begin to develop and grow mentally while others may not grow at the same rate. You find yourself not able to have some of the same conversations that you used to have.

You may have heard the phrase, "you've changed," from old acquaintances. To them your conversation now is contradictory to what it once was. This is a great compliment if you have grown in a positive manner. Your friends and family want you to stay consistent. This makes communicating with you easy. Never changing, especially your thinking, makes you more predictable.

As you grow mentally and have new experiences and learn new ideas and concepts you are going to have to separate yourself from certain people. This doesn't mean you love them any less or that you are better than them. It simply means that in order to implement and take action on what you are learning you will need to have people that understand your level of growth close to you. You cannot have people who hold you back or speak negatively about what you desire in your space. They will hinder your growth and block your path.

There are people in my life that I was close with in the past, but today I don't interact with them like I used to. It's not because we are not friends anymore, it's that our paths have taken us in different directions. If I see them while I'm out or we talk on the phone we will have a great conversation and catch up. But our time together will be limited. We will show each other love and we will go on with our life.

To avoid making people uncomfortable, most people slip back into their old thinking. They attempt to go back to an old mindset they no longer embody. The majority of the time, this is done to not make the other person feel weird. We don't want people that we had relationships with in the past to look at us like we have changed. So, we dummy down our growth. We have a phony conversation, that doesn't represent how much we have mentally grown over time.

What you may not realize is that your contradiction may just be what someone needs to get inspired to make a change in their life. Many people today are looking for a sign, a sign that confirms that they should do something different. There may be something that they have been struggling with and your story can help them make the commitment to move in a new direction.

Recently a visit to my doctor exposed a health issue for me. This was a surprise and was eye opening. Due to this issue I had to have surgery. Any time surgery is involved it is a drastic life experience. When I found out about this I started to do some research. I found that one of my issues was what and how I ate. So, I decided to change my diet and eating habits. I made a major change.

It was summer time and my wife and I loved to cookout and have family and friends over. I enjoyed a good hamburger, Italian sausage on the grill and my mother's potato salad. (She makes THE BEST potato salad on the planet. And it's not even up for debate.) As part of my change in eating, I decided to cut those things out of my diet.

Some of my close friends and family know of the changes I have made. Somewhat surprisingly, my change in diet has inspired some of our friends and family to look at what and how they eat. Because I am now contradicting what I used to say I liked to eat, others are being inspired. This was not something that I tried to convince others that they needed to do in their life.

When you have a conversation with someone, what you say is based on what you know and believe at that time. If you speak with that person again at a later date about the same topic you may feel differently. During the time between the first conversation and the next conversation you learned some new things, you have new experiences and insights and now your opinion is different. Are you contradicting what you previously said? Yes. Is that a problem? No.

Here is a question for you to ponder: If your thinking doesn't change on certain topics are you growing?

The bible makes reference to this, (I'm not preaching just teaching) 1st Corinthians 13:11 states "when I was a child, I spoke like a child, I thought like a child, I reasoned like a child. When I became a man, I set aside childish ways." As you grow (especially mentally) you will have to set aside old ways and thinking. This is the natural transition of growth.

When I was in college, at North Carolina A & T, "Aggie Pride", I had a purpose and a reason why I was there. That reason was to get a college education and earn a degree. I was 315 miles away from home, I was free, no parents watching me, no curfew and I was 17 years old when I first got there. My thinking at the time was "I'm going to get it in" we are going to party every weekend, and sometimes during the week too. I will do some work so I don't get kicked out and keep my parents off my back. For me, being at an HBCU that had a slight reputation as a party school my thinking was party, party, then squeeze in some time to study.

We had what we called 2 to 6's. This was a party that didn't start until 2am and was over at 6am. We were hype when they had 2-6's. We knew that it was an all-night party. So, we would start early in the evening and just hang out until 2am. I loved it. We would get our party on then leave around 5 or 6 in the morning go to IHOP and have breakfast. We would get back to our dorm and sleep most of the next day. I believed that was the life! (I did do enough work to earn my degree, I didn't just party the entire time)

If someone asked me today to go to a party that didn't start until 2am, I would look at them like they lost their mind. My wife and I laugh now because on Friday or Saturday night we will be in the house and by 10:30pm – 11:00pm we are looking at each other like "I'm going to bed."

At 17-18 years old, I thought that not having anybody monitoring my actions was freedom. I could do what I wanted. At the time that meant going out and not having someone telling me what time to be home. Now, as a grown man with kids, I want to be home. I'm not looking to be out all night. I have a different outlook and meaning of being free. I loved my college experience, but I have mentally grown and would not do or talk about the same things I did in college.

My conversation with one of my college buddies today would be a direct contradiction to what it was back then. I tell you this story because my thinking today SHOULD be a contradiction to my thinking when I was 17 years old. And so should yours.

We can't live our lives in fear of making others feel uncomfortable because we have changed and grown. People hide how their thoughts may have changed because those they associate with still feel the same way they always have. With mental growth comes new feelings, new thoughts and new actions.

What are you Thinking?

I would caution you that we are talking about contradicting your old thinking, but this is only beneficial if you are making positive changes. If your mindset is going in the negative direction you must understand your actions will be negative as well. So, let's be clear that your mindset dictates your actions and your actions determine the direction you go in life. When you contradict yourself make sure you are changing for the better.

What should you take away from this chapter? First, is the understanding that if you are growing you will contradict what you thought and believed in the past. Second, you can't dummy down your higher level of knowledge and understanding. And third, you are not here to make everyone feel comfortable by not showing who you really are and who you have become.

Contradicting yourself is part of being human!

Ideas to implement to become a Constant Contradiction.

1. **Examine what you believe** – I'm not talking about your religious beliefs, but what you believe about yourself. What you believe about your abilities. What you believe about why you are here. As you examine these and other things about yourself, I encourage you to challenge those beliefs.
2. **Focus on Growth** – You will not just fall into the place you want to be. You won't go to bed one night and wake up a new person with new thoughts and ideas. You will have to focus on learning and having new experiences that will give you the

insights, skills and knowledge to accomplish what you desire in life. Make this a priority.
3. **Make decisions based on what you want to accomplish** – This one may seem basic and common sense, but this is not what most people do. Be alright with people being uncomfortable with you changing. Be a little selfish when making decisions. Make them based on what you need and want to accomplish and you will have a larger impact than trying to please a few.

20

Why Me?

Small thinking begins with questioning why you are being challenged.

In life you may have situations that arise that lead you to ask the question: "Why Me?" These are typically situations that you don't find favorable. When they happen your thoughts usually become those of defense and denial. Your self-talk begins to sound like this: "What did I do to deserve this?" "Why do bad things always happen to me?" "This is the worst day of my life." "What did I do wrong?"

When you ask, "why me," it implies that you are relieving yourself of any involvement in what has taken place. You accept the role of the victim. By no means am I proclaiming that you have control over every event that occurs in life. What I am asserting is that you have 100% control over how you perceive and respond to the event.

Life is nothing more than a series of events. When you get a promotion on your job, start a new business, lose a loved one, or get into a car accident your brain instantly evaluates the event based on past experiences. Depending on how you viewed similar events before, you will label what just happened as good or bad. The event itself is not predestined as either, you create the category it goes in.

Something that most people don't realize is that how you think about life events determines how you feel about them. And how you feel about the event determines how you respond. If you don't take a moment to pause and think about what has happened, the impact of the event can be greater than it has to be. The only way for you to have an outcome that is desirable, is to create a response that will yield that type of outcome. The default action for most is to just react without thinking.

What I know to be true, is that as soon as you accept the phrase "why me" you turn your focus to everything that is not going the way you would like. You begin to focus on what could be going wrong. Your amygdala is in full control and has highjacked your brain. In this mental state, the resources necessary to operate your prefrontal cortex, the CEO of the brain, are unavailable. This makes it difficult to see the good in your current situation and think logically and creatively.

Most people go down the path of "why me", not because it will help the situation, but because it will distract from the situation. When you get "bad" news, the only thing asking the question "why me" will do is distract you from realizing what you need to do next. Your brain kicks into fight, flight or flee mode to keep you safe. Why me is a distraction method your brain uses to protect you. It wants to avoid the pain of reality and distract you from focusing on the issue at hand.

But no matter how hard you fight, how "safe" you try to play it, you won't be able to avoid every situation. You will feel pain, you will feel discomfort, you will find yourself in a position that you would rather not be in. The question at that moment should not be "why me?" It should be "What Now?" "What am I supposed to learn?" Every situation you find yourself in is a teachable moment, a character-building moment or simply a blessing.

I want you to take a second and think back over your life and recall that moment when you may have been in a situation and you asked yourself "why me?" In that moment, do you believe that if you got the answer to that question, it would have changed the situation? Now I want you to think about what lesson you may have missed by focusing on "why me?"

One thing you must understand is that where your focus goes your energy flows. If you allow your thoughts to dwell on the "bad" news you receive you will not be in the mindset of finding the blessing or lesson from the situation. I will admit, this is difficult. It can be a challenge to get what could be considered "bad" news and focus on what good could come from it.

The question "why me?" is never answered when asked. If I asked, to whom are you actually asking the question, most people would say they are asking God or the Universe. In a situation of stress or duress you may seek an answer to this question. You may even look to a higher power for answers and that is understandable. But if you think about it, how many times have you received an answer directly to this question when you asked?

The answer to this question can only come in hindsight. As you look back over what has transpired in your life and you recall an event, then can you make sense of why you were in that situation. You can only connect the dots looking back. When you think about that moment when you asked, why me, you now can see how the event made an impact.

In the summer of 2017, I went to the doctor because I wasn't feeling 100%. After a few tests and procedures, it was discovered that I had a mass growing in my colon. Here is where I could have easily asked the dreaded question: **"Why Me?"** Followed by "What? What does that mean doc?" How could this be? I thought I was eating pretty good. I had a gym membership. I'm not on any medications, I'm not a sickly person. I walk a lot. I drink plenty of water. Now, I did like my cigars, but I didn't smoke a pack of cigarettes a day. How did this happen? What did I do to deserve this? I was only 46 years old.

I could have tumbled down the rabbit hole of becoming defensive, being in denial and asked why me? But that would not have changed the fact that I had a mass in my colon. Even if I had found exactly why this mass started to grow, it still would not have changed the fact that it was there.

The next phase is usually the trap of comparison. You start to look at others and what they are doing in their life and you compare what you have been doing. You say, they are doing things that are much worst. They don't eat as healthy as I do. All kinds of self-talk, comparing your actions and activities with someone else's actions and activities. This leads down the rabbit hole too and you lose yourself.

Prior to this event, I had been working on my mind and mindset for many years. Now I'm hit with some news that could be life changing and even devastating. It was test time! Does all this mindset, positive affirmations and awareness stuff really work?

I was a believer. But, when something happens that would, to most people, give them reason to question it, I didn't. I believe that our brains are phenomenal machines and our bodies follow and react to our thoughts. My goal was to make sure that my thinking was in direct correlation to what I wanted the outcome to be. Every thought I had went through the equation E+R=O (Event + Response = Outcome.)

While my wife and I sat there with the doctor and he was telling us about this mass they found, all I could think about was my response. I knew that my Response had to dictate what Outcome I wanted. At this point I had no control over the Event, but I had 100% control over my Response.

So, I asked, "what do we do next?" The doctor's response was, we operate. We need to get it out before it grows and causes more problems. Wow...surgery...ok. This was new for me. I had never been operated on before. But it is what it is at this point. When can we do this? Our next step was to meet with the surgeon and discuss the details and schedule the surgery.

Here we are, the day of surgery. I have done all the prep work I was instructed to do and now we are ready. My mindset is: Let's get this started so we can get it over with.

The surgeon comes to talk with us before we start and, he explains the procedure and the risk of surgery again. After his talk I kiss my wife and they roll me into the OR. It's showtime!

After it's over the doctor tells my wife everything went well. They are going to send what they removed to the lab to be tested. This is a surgery they usually do when people have Cancer. Yep…Cancer, capital C. The doctor comes to my room in the hospital a couple days later with the results. He has this baffled look on his face. Then he begins to tell me that everything went well. I was doing good and he says your results are back and you DO NOT HAVE CANCER!

He was baffled because he believed that I did, just looking at what they removed. Can I be transparent with you? I never, not once during this entire process, ever thought I had cancer. That literally was not a thought that even crossed my mind.

Earlier in this chapter I mentioned that there is a lesson, a teachable moment and/or blessing in every situation. What could I have possibly learned or been blessed with in this situation. Well there were multiple things. First, the blessing was NO CANCER! I don't have to see any doctors moving forward, I don't have to take any medication and I can go on with my life as if this had never happened, and I have. The lesson for me was that I need to be more vigilant about what I put in my body. I made a life decision and changed what I eat.

Here is another thing that was revealed to me. The principles and concepts that I teach, were confirmed. We do have an amazing power to think ourselves into the situations we want to be in. You have more power and control than you may believe. Every day from the moment I heard the news that there was a mass in my colon until the day of the surgery I would meditate. During my meditation time I would sweep the mass out of my colon. I would visualize it moving and being gone. What is so phenomenal about this is that the surgeon told me that he didn't see the mass while operating. What once was the mass had blended into my colon took the shape of my colon and literally was not what it was before. I don't know what you may believe, but I believe I was blessed and I had something to do with that.

As I look back and connect the dots. I now have an amazing story to tell. I thought my story was good before, but now it is truly compelling. It slowed me down to take a minute to think about what I wanted from life. During this time, I decided to finally write this book. I don't believe I would have moved with urgency if I didn't have this event occur. Sometimes what you go through is not for you, it is so that you can tell your story. And your story can move someone else can into action. Stories move people. And YOUR STORY MATTERS.

You may or may not have gone through a dramatic life event. You may have lost your job, maybe you are in the middle of a divorce, you may have lost a loved one, or maybe you were overlooked for that promotion. Whatever it is, understand this, the reason people say "When life gives you lemons, make lemonade," is because people have been in situations that didn't look good and they turned them into the blessing that they were designed to be.

Moving forward in your journey, when you are in a situation and you want to ask, "Why me," be conscious and use that moment as a prompt to remind you that the universe is in teaching mode. There is something that you need to learn that will be of use to you in the future. Shift away from the mindset of the victim.

When you find yourself in a difficult situation ask yourself **"Why not me?"** If I had not gone through what I went through I would not have a compelling story to share. It would not have confirmed for me, that our mindset and thinking truly play a part in the outcome of situations that occur in our life. You can only connect the dots looking back.

──────────────── *What Now* ────────────────

Instead of asking "Why me?"

1. Change your perception of what you go through.
2. Live your life by E+R=O.
3. Be of the mindset that where your focus goes your energy flows.

21
Coincidence or Confirmation

The Universe will send you confirmation that you are on the right path, but to most it looks like a coincidence.

We have all had that moment when something happens and we say, "what a coincidence." If we look deeper at the event, was it a coincidence or was it confirmation?

The root word for Coincidence is the Latin word Coincidere (Coincide) – it means to occur at or during the same time. Occur simultaneously, happen together. Here is a definition that I love and I think is true to what actually happens - Coincidence - **Incidences cooperating with each other. Vibrational harmony.**

When you think of something being a coincidence it is nothing more than the Universe bringing us to a place that we need to be. And at the same time, it shows us what we need to see (or hear) based on what we stated we wanted. When you speak you are putting out into the Universe what it is that you want. The Universe accepts what you say and goes to work to make it happen. This may not show itself right away and it may not show up how you expect it. But, when the pieces of the puzzle are shown people say, "What a coincidence."

During an episode of an internet radio show I used to host, called "WiseWordsWithDarius," I was sharing how our amygdala sometimes highjacks our pre-frontal cortex. At the time I was on the air doing the show, my wife Allison, was taking a class at Georgetown University. After the show, she sent me a text message with a few pictures of the slides that the professor was showing based on what they were discussing. Now, Allison knew what I was going to be discussing on that episode of the show. The pics that she sent were slides talking about what happens when your amygdala highjacks your pre-frontal cortex. Her professor was covering the exact same topic at the same time I was talking about it on my show.

Would you say that was a coincidence? I wouldn't, and I didn't. My first thought was, I am on point with what I am sharing. This was confirmation for me, not coincidence. I had been putting out in the Universe that I wanted to bring enlightenment and knowledge to everyone who hears me speak. I want to share thought-provoking ideas and success principles and how they work, backed by neuroscience to my audiences. Those text messages sent by my wife confirmed the following for me: 1. I am putting out great content (if they are teaching it at Georgetown University I accept it as being great content) and 2. that which I am sharing is relevant and people are looking for this information. Furthermore, those that were in her class paid thousands of dollars to be a part of that course. This gave me the confirmation that I needed, to know I was on the right path.

Why do these occurrences happen? These so-called "coincidences" happen when you are in harmonious vibration with what you say you want, and what the Universe wants for you. Everything is in a constant state of vibration. How you feel is based on your vibration at that time. It may be a positive vibration, when you feel good, or a negative vibration when you are not feeling so good.

Here is what you need to understand. When you make plans, the Universe makes plans for you. Once you are in the right vibration, confirmations happen to let you know you on the right track. This is like tuning a piano. You tune a piano by making adjustments to the tension of the strings so they create a certain vibration. Based on the key you are tuning, you match it to the sound that key makes on a piano tuner. Once they are on the same vibration that key is tuned.

This is the same concept that applies to your journey. When you have a goal, you must make sure your actions and thoughts are on the same vibration as what you want to accomplish. This means you must be conscious of your vibration. Be aware of how you are feeling and if you are getting the confirmations you need to move forward.

Your level of vibration is powerful. It will bring to you what you put out. Have you ever had a thought of somebody and then you either run into that person while you're out or they call you? I'm pretty sure we all have. Was that a coincidence? Or was it confirmation? Your vibration was in perfect harmony with that person. And what makes us look at it as a "coincidence" is that we may not have realized that they either needed us or we needed them at that specific time.

Let me throw a wrinkle in this thinking. There will be times when you put things out and the Universe will send somebody to you that you never thought would have the answers you were looking for. When this happens and you are not paying attention you will miss your help.

In August of 2008, I was sitting at a bar with a friend. Around that time, I was getting my life in order. I was single and starting to enjoy myself. But I was having thoughts of finding someone to build a life with. I had no one in mind for this position. As the evening went on a group of ladies sat down at the bar right next to me. I didn't think much of it until one of the ladies who was standing behind me kept trying to get the bar tenders attention. As she would lean in she was putting her boobs on my head and shoulder. So, I asked her if she needed me to get the bar tender for her. Now don't get me wrong, I like boobs, but not when they are randomly put on my head.

Out the corner of my eye I saw a face I thought was familiar. I wasn't sure so I casually looked again. I said to the young lady standing behind me "I know your friend over there." This was my way of being sure that it was who I thought it was before I embarrassed myself. She said "who?" I said her (covertly pointing), her name is Allison, right? Not knowing who I was dealing with, she blurted out "Allison you know him?" Pointing at me.

Yep, it was Allison. This was a girl I dated in high school. We talked and exchanged information before we left. Two years later we were married.

I am living the life that I wanted, but I had no thought or idea that it would be with Allison. She never crossed my mind. We were always cool in school but she wasn't on my radar. This is how the Universe works. You put something out there and it will send someone who has the answer. But that someone may not be the person you thought it would be.

This is why I repeatedly say, "Pay Attention!" If you are not paying attention or you are applying your biases to what is happening in your life you will miss your answer.

There is so much help around you that you miss because you're letting conditions be what you are reacting to instead of the vibrations that you deliberately created be what you respond to. The issue is that most people are creating their life by default. They are letting what they are observing set the tone, instead of setting their tone and watching what comes. This is what happens when we React and not Respond.

The most convoluted trail is the path of least resistance. In your mind, you have these things you want to accomplish or achieve, but because of how you are programmed you don't believe 100%. So, you put out these thoughts of resistance. They start out as limiting beliefs and negative self-talk. The Universe doesn't say "there is too much resistance let's just give it up." The Universe says, "Oh that's how they want it, let's give them what they want."

If things are happening in your life that you don't like or desire, take a step back and think about the vibrations you are putting out into the Universe. The Universe is only giving you back what you put out. Everything that unfolds is the explanation of what your habit of vibration is in relationship to what your vibration of desire is. The Universe responds to powerful desire.

If you are not conscious and aware of your thoughts you may be putting a lot of power in what you don't want. If your thoughts are constantly focused on all the things that you don't want or don't want to happen, the Universe has no choice but to give you what you are focusing on and giving power to.

When the Universe responds to what we put out (and sometimes this may be instantly or it may be years later based on what's active in your vibration) here is how most people respond. **They Justify when things don't go their way and they Testify when they do.**

When they have those "coincidences" happen that don't work in their favor they are quick to give reasons and excuses as to why these things are happening to them. They will blame others and circumstances, they ignore what is happening, and they don't take any responsibility. People point the finger at everyone but themselves. But if it goes their way, they pull out their soapbox step up on it and shout to the masses how great things are and how they are making it happen.

Here is the truth: **Things are happening just the way you set them up**. If things are going well or not going so well, you set it up. There is no such thing as coincidence. Simply put, you have orchestrated the plan that the Universe follows to create your life.

What Now

Here is the Mindset you need to have to recognize your confirmations.

1. **Tell yourself: Things are always working out for me.** When things happen along the way let them happen. When you look back at them you will see that they were opportunities for you.
2. **Respond to conditions.** Consciously take a moment to Respond rather than unconsciously React. Deliberately put out what you want from life. Set the tone and observe what happens.
3. **Change your vibration.** Everything is in a state of vibration. Your vibration plays a part in what you attract. If you are in a negative vibration alter your thoughts and emotions.

About the Author

By the age of 25, Darius Wise had been arrested twice, was drowning in debt, and fathered a son while in a relationship with no future. Raised in a two-parent, upper middle-class home that was rooted in fundamental moral values anchored by religious belief, he never imagined his life would be mired by situations like these. With positive intervention and introspection, less than a decade later, his life underwent a 180-degree turn. Humbled by the experience, he realized the importance of reaching out and redirecting adults as well as today's youth—and not only those identified as at-risk—to divert them away from pathways that lead to despair. He encourages everyone that he is in contact with to dream, explore and embrace their journey while simultaneously understanding the correlation between thoughts and actions.

During his twenties, Darius admits that he didn't fully understand that correlation. He simply made assumptions about what his life would be based on his upbringing. His hard-working parents provided a comfortable existence for their two children. The Wise's planned, saved and prepared for their college educations. And similar to most parents, they imagined a level of success for those children that superseded their own. So, at 25, Darius questioned why his life was plunging in the opposite direction?

He readily shares how poor decisions, immaturity and thinking charm and empty words would be the salve for every rough spot he encountered were the culprit. Thankfully, none of these derailed his one must-do mission—graduating from college. However, graduating was not the launching pad for Darius' success.
The wakeup call came a few years later in the form of a mentor who challenged his short-sighted thinking and introduced Darius to the benefits of achieving emotional and financial wealth. Empowered with a purpose, he began to discover books that explored how our thoughts and beliefs determine our actions and, in turn, impact our results. In a span of approximately three years, he eliminated his debt and launched a few unsuccessful businesses, but he was not derailed from his quest for financial wealth.

But most importantly, his emotional wealth had grown exponentially and because of this his behaviors and actions had changed. The sum of Darius' experiences, realizations and transformations inspired him to help others reach their full potential. He set his sights on becoming a motivational speaker—studying the teachings of many dynamic orators and, eventually, joined their ranks.

Today, this husband and father of four has over 25 years of teaching experience in adult education where he has trained employees from local and federal government agencies and private sector in addition to inspiring entrepreneurs. Darius

About the Author

holds a Master Facilitator certification from The Association of Talent Development (ATD), is a Microsoft-Certified Professional, a Jack Canfield Certified Trainer and he received his NeuroCoach certification from the OptiMind Neuroscience Coaching & Training Institute. He was an invited keynote speaker for the Maryland public school system and the Johns Hopkins women's basketball team. He was the recipient of the "Outstanding Presentation and Keynote" certificate from the National Capitol area Kiwanis Club. Darius has also been a featured speaker for The Director's Conference, New Co-op Communicators Conference, and the PowerUp Admin conference sponsored by the National Rural Electric Cooperative Association.

Hundreds of listeners tuned in every Saturday morning to hear Darius' weekly Blog Talk Radio show "#WiseWordsWithDarius," where he offered thought-provoking insights and success principles that provide practical life skills for making sound day-to-day decisions and achieving dreams. He believes and teaches others that understanding why we make the decisions we make is key to reducing our missteps and regrets.

Darius is also the founder and CEO of WiseDecisions, LLC, an organization committed to preparing individuals to focus on the mindset necessary to face life's challenges. The mission is to teach his audiences how to take control of their phenomenal brain and consciously use it every day to achieve their life goals.

Darius is a proud graduate of North Carolina Agricultural and Technical State University - "Aggie Pride" and holds a Bachelor of Science (B.S.) in Industrial Technology.

Darius "The Professor" Wise Wants to Hear from You

Tell Darius how *"What Are You Thinking"* has impacted your life.

E-mail Darius at info@IAmDariusWise.com

Or

Send written correspondence to:
WiseDecisions, LLC
What Are You Thinking Feedback
9103 Woodmore Centre Dr
Suite 348
Lanham, Md 20706

Get more training, insights, videos, resources and upcoming live event info at:
www.IAmDariusWise.com

Connect with @DariusAWise on social media

Book Darius to speak at your next event at:
www.IAmDariusWise.com/Book-Darius